AMARNA
City of Akhenaten and Nefertiti

AMARNA

City of Akhenaten and Nefertiti

Key pieces from the Petrie Collection

Petrie Museum

Julia Samson

With an Introduction by Professor H. S. Smith

Published for the Department of Egyptology
University College, London.

To the Department of Egyptology at University College, London, past
and present, with gratitude and affection

". . . the business of life is to endeavour to find out what you don't know
by what you do."—Arthur Wellesley, Duke of Wellington, 1769-1852.

ISBN 0 85668 000 1

Set in 12 on 14pt Monotype Bembo
and printed on 140 g.s.m. B.20 Beaublade
Designed by Peter Elek
Printed in Great Britain by
Biddles Limited, Martyr Road, Guildford, Surrey

Contents

LIST OF PLATES

N.B. Facsimiles of the colour plates have been added for ease of reference where appropriate.

Acknowledgements

My gratitude, as unending as his patience has been, goes to Professor H. S. Smith who suggested this book in the first place and who has envisaged and stimulated a series of works on the material in the Museum as a whole. He has been my unfailing mentor throughout, but none of the views expressed in the book should be laid at his door. The project was started under the benign aegis of Professor Emery whose sad loss we all deplore. During the writing of the book I have had unstinting assistance both in this country and abroad for which I want to express my warmest appreciation to all those who have helped.

In particular I wish to thank Dr. Eiddon Edwards, Keeper of the Department of Egyptian Antiquities at the British Museum for allowing me to see their store collection, and his assistants for sparing their valuable time. Dr. P. R. S. Moorey, Assistant Keeper of the Department of Antiquities, Ashmolean Museum, Oxford, gave me every facility to work in the Department, handle the Petrie material there and study the store collection for which I am very grateful to him and his helpful staff. My warm appreciation, too, goes to M. Jacques Vandier, Conservateur en chef du Départment des Antiquités égyptiennes au Musée du Louvre for his kindness, and the determined help of his assistants who under strike conditions secured for me all the facilities I needed.

I am very grateful to the late Dr. William Stevenson Smith, then Curator of the Department of Egyptian Art, Museum of Fine Arts, Boston, and Dr. John D. Cooney, Curator of Egyptian and Classical Art at the Cleveland Museum of Art, for their helpful documentation. Dr. Nicholas Fintzelberg, Chief Curator, San Diego Museum of Man, kindly sent photographs of the 'princess' figures in that collection, which were admirably supplemented by the drawings of my co-operative colleague Miss Joyce Townend, on a visit to the States.

The great majority of the photographs in the book are the result of the time and trouble spent in the College Central Photographic Service for which my very full appreciation goes to Mr. E. Hitchcock and his skilful assistants. To this I add my gratitude to Dr. S. K. Mathews of the Ealing School of Photography, and his willing assistants for the plates they so ably contributed.

For illustrations other than those of objects in the College I want to thank the Griffith Institute, Oxford, for plates 42, 14b and Miss Helen Murray for her promptitude; the Ashmolean Museum for plate 9; the Louvre for plate 5b and Dr. Henry Riad, Director of the Cairo Museum for allowing the use of the plates of the Cairo fragment of the coregency stela, plate 55c, and those of Tutankhamen's ivory box lid and golden throne, plates 42 and 14b. Thanks for the photographs of the Berlin heads of Nefertiti go to the Staatliche Museen, Berlin. The Egypt Exploration Society has kindly permitted the use of the map (plate A) from *The City of Akhenaten*, Part *II*, and the plan and elevation of the city (plates B and C) from *The City of Akhenaten*, Part *III*. I should like also to thank Miss Ann Petrie who has been exceedingly helpful in arranging access to her father's unpublished Journal from the site.

I am grateful to Dr. Andrée Rosenfeld of the British Museum for her advice on the current nomenclature of the stones used in the Ancient World. In the Petrie Museum my special appreciation for on-the-spot help goes to Dr. David Dixon, Curator, and Mrs. Adams; and in the Department to Dr. Geoffrey Martin for time spent away from his own work on objects from the Amarna royal tomb; to the Secretary of the Department Miss Anthea Page for her absolutely vital initiative; and to Dr. Rosalie David for the vigilant and searching eye she cast over the manuscript. At home my heartfelt thanks goes to Alison King for her unfailing encouragement and generous and imaginative help.

JULIA SAMSON   March 1972

ABBREVIATIONS

AKK & G	H. Muller, *Ägyptische Kunstwerke, Kleinfunde und Glas*, Berlin, 1964.
AEG and G	Elizabeth Riefstahl, *Ancient Egyptian Glass and Glazes*, Brooklyn Museum, 1968.
Ashmolean	Ashmolean Museum, Oxford.
B.M.	British Museum, London.
Cairo	Cairo Egyptian Museum, Cairo.
C/A	*The City of Akhenaten*, part 1, T. E. Peet, C. L. Woolley and others, 1923; Part II, H. Frankfort, J. D. S. Pendlebury and H. W. Fairman, 1933; Part III, Vol. I Text, Vol. II plates, J. D. S. Pendlebury, J. Cerny, H. W. Fairman, H. Frankfort, L. Murray Thriepland and J. Samson, 1951. All are published by the E.E.S., London, W.C.1.
CCG	Cairo Catalogue Général.
E.E.S.	Egypt Exploration Society, London, W.C.1.
J.E.A.	Journal of Egyptian Archaeology, E.E.S., London.
M.D.O.G.	Mitteilungen der Deutchen Orient-Gesellschaft-Berlin, 1911/12; 1912/13; 1913/14; 1917.
MMA	Metropolitan Museum of Art, New York, U.S.A.
P. T/A	W. M. Flinders Petrie, *Tell el-Amarna*, London, 1894.
Rec. de Mons. Egyptienne	J. Capart, Recueil de monuments égyptiens, Brussels, 1905.
RTA	N. de Garis Davis, The Rock Tombs of El Amarna, 6 volumes, 1903, 1905 (2), 1906, 1908 (2), The Egypt Exploration Fund (now Society), London.
Vandier Manuel d'Archaéologie	J. Vandier, Manuel d'Archéologie Égyptienne, III, Paris, 1958.
Z.A.S.	Zeitschrift für Ägyptische Sprache, Leipzig. . . .

Introduction
by H. S. Smith

The purpose of this book is to illustrate and discuss the finest works from the site of Tell el-Amarna in the Petrie Museum in the Department of Egyptology at University College London. This museum primarily comprises the private collection of Egyptian antiquities excavated and purchased by the late Sir W. M. Flinders Petrie during his long and distinguished archaeological career in Egypt. It was acquired by the College in 1913. To it have been added generous gifts, notably that of the Egyptian Collection of the late Sir Henry Wellcome by his Trustees in 1964. The Petrie Museum is utilised by the Department of Egyptology in its teaching and research, but its collections are made available to outside scholars and students and are open to the public. Petrie himself published a large part, but not all, of his collection. This volume is the first of a number of works designed to complete this great task.

Tell el-Amarna is the modern name of the site of the ancient Egyptian city of Akhetaten, "The Horizon of Aten". It is situated on the east bank in a great bay of hills formed by the cliffs of the eastern desert, near Deir Mowas in Middle Egypt about half-way between Cairo and Luxor. In the middle of the fourteenth century B.C. Pharaoh Akhenaten chose this virgin site to be a new royal residence and capital city of all Egypt, and to be the centre of the state-cult of the sun-god in the form of Aten, "the Sun-disk". The city with its temples, palaces, state buildings and great private mansions was soon built, and Akhenaten moved in with his Queen, Nefertiti and his court. The cult of the sun was the sole official cult in the city, in contrast to the normal Egyptian practice of worshipping many gods under many different forms. Akhenaten, "The Spirit of Aten" and his family were the principal devotees of the cult, in the universality of which Akhenaten came to believe to such an extent that late in his reign he gave orders for the names of all other gods to be chiselled out of temple inscriptions and monuments all over Egypt. This action has caused him to be spoken of by various writers as the world's first monotheist, as a great religious reformer and revolutionary, as the "heretic" Pharaoh, or as an insane religious fanatic. After Akhenaten's death, his successor Tutankhaten fairly soon returned to the traditional capital of Thebes, restored the state cult of Amen-Re and changed his name to Tutankhamen; the cults of Egypt's traditional gods were officially recognised once more. Akhetaten was abandoned. At some time after this, the name of Akhenaten was officially pronounced anathema, and he was referred to as "the fallen one of Akhetaten". The temples he had built to the Aten all over Egypt were razed to the ground, figures and inscriptions of Akhenaten and his god were hammered out on all public monuments, and the city of

Map of Egypt (Plate 56)

1

Akhetaten was demolished and despoiled, never to be re-inhabited.

Because of their unusual history, Akhenaten and his city have provoked great public interest during recent years. The material from Tell el-Amarna described in this book is of outstanding artistic and scientific interest, because, with the exception of four pieces from the Wellcome Collection, it was all bought or excavated by Petrie in his pioneer excavation at the site in 1891-92. Unlike much Amarna art purchased on the antiquities market and published in recent years, Petrie's materials have a known and detailed provenance and their authenticity cannot be called into question. Their special importance is that they mostly came from the largest and most impressive building at Amarna, the Great Palace, which was unique in its plan and its lavish polychrome decoration. Though subsequent excavation at Amarna by the Deutsche Orient Gesellschaft before the first war and the Egypt Exploration Society between the wars yielded buildings of great importance, none rivals the Great Palace in its scale nor in the decorative techniques used. In his excavation report, *Tell el-Amarna* (1894), Petrie published many of his finds; the work was remarkable for its time. However, only a proportion of even the finest objects were illustrated, and these in photographs that do them no justice: and his descriptions were summary. In view of the exceptional intrinsic interest of the art of Amarna, and the fact that it is the only ancient Egyptian city which has been at all thoroughly excavated, full publication of Petrie's material is of prime importance.

The author of this work, Mrs. Julia Samson, commenced study of Petrie's Amarna collection under Professor S. R. K. Glanville in 1934, and produced a chapter concerning it in the Egypt Exploration Society's publication *City of Akhenaten*, Vol. III. She returned to the Egyptology Department at University College in 1966 as an Honorary Research Associate. She has done me the honour of asking me to contribute to her book a sketch of the historical background to the discoveries at Tell el-Amarna for those readers unfamiliar with ancient Egyptian history. Many interesting works, both learned and speculative, have been written in recent years about the exceptional problems which Amarna history raises. The summary that follows attempts only to present what is reasonably well established, without argument or discussion of evidence.

HISTORY

The reign of Akhenaten's father, Amenophis III (*c.* 1405-1368 B.C.) was peaceful and prosperous. Egypt's client states in Palestine and Syria, which had been brought under her sway by the conqueror Tuthmosis III in the mid-fifteenth century, though they might intrigue against one another, were serving Egypt's interests under the watchful eyes of Egyptian legates. A temporary balance of power between Egypt, the Hurrian state of Mitanni, the Hittites, the Assyrians and the Babylonians had been achieved by judicious use of Egypt's gold, by diplomacy and dynastic marriages. Never had imported luxuries from the Levant and the Aegean world flowed into Egypt in more profusion. In the south Egypt had secured her frontier beyond

Map of Egypt (Plate 56)

2

the Fourth Cataract, and Amenophis was building great Egyptian temple cities along the fertile Dongola bend to create a new province. In Egypt itself, Amenophis had built for himself and his Great Royal Wife Ty a splendid palace at Malkata in western Thebes (opposite modern Luxor) in which to celebrate their jubilees, and an enormous mortuary temple beside it. Temples were founded, restored and extended both at Thebes, the capital, and throughout the country. The endowments for these were munificent, more especially for the great temple of Karnak at Thebes, the seat of the state god Amen-Re. Full temple treasuries and granaries in Egypt meant not only the ability to withstand bad Nile years and the long summer droughts, but the capacity to bring new land under cultivation and to stimulate craftsmanship and artistic production. Priests and state officials were richly rewarded for their services by the King, and were able to build for themselves fine town-houses and villas, with large estates to support them. Our sources tell us little of the common people, but they can hardly have failed to benefit in some ways from the stable economic and agricultural conditions, and the availability of work on state projects during the barren months of the year.

At this time, though the ancient cults of Egypt's gods flourished and prospered in their cities and their priesthoods had become virtually a professional body, yet the state cult of Amen-Re had been endowed with so large a proportion of Egypt's agricultural land and received such large annual imposts from the Pharaoh's dependencies in the north and south that its position was paramount, and it functioned as an arm of the state executive. Amen was the patron god of the Theban XVIIIth Dynasty to which Amenophis belonged. During the fifteenth century, his cult became ever more fused with that of the sun-god Re, whose foremost cult city was at On (Heliopolis), north of modern Cairo and near the great administrative and military capital at Memphis. The sun-god was the lord of the universe, the creator of gods and mankind, and the giver of all life and its benefits. The king ruled this world according to Re's divine plans by virtue of being his son. During the reigns of Amenophis III's grandfather Amenophis II and his father Tuthmosis IV, an ever-increasing number of hymns and prayers to the sun-god as the giver of life were composed and inscribed on stelae, tomb-doors, and other monuments. Though the sun-god is addressed in his Heliopolitan form of Re-Harakhty (Horus of the Horizons), he is occasionally referred to in these hymns as Aten, the disk of the sun. The growth of sun cult has been plausibly attributed in part to the results of contact with the religions of the Levant after Tuthmosis III's conquests, but this cannot be proved; we should know more if Heliopolis had been excavated.

An Egyptian crown prince in the XVIIIth Dynasty was regularly married to the eldest daughter of the reigning king and his chief Queen. This princess was known as the God's Wife of Amen, and became the Great Royal Wife when the crown prince succeeded; her children alone were considered to be born of the god, and had the prime right of succession. But Amenophis III made Ty, daughter of the priest Yuya and his wife Tuyu, neither of whom apparently were of royal stock, his Great Royal Wife. Ty's name, unlike that of earlier queens, is regularly placed in a cartouche and included in royal titularies; and she is represented as of equivalent stature with the King—sure marks that she held exceptional power and influence. Prince Amenhotep (Akhenaten's birth name) was born of this union. Of his early years there is virtually no record; presumably he was brought up by a tutor in the royal residences at Thebes and elsewhere, being educated in court ritual, the arts of government, warfare and the royal sports. Before he ascended the throne he was married to Nefertiti, whose parentage is unknown; on the basis of her name, which means "the beautiful one who is come" it has been suggested that she may have been the Mitannian princess Tadukhipa; but this is unsupported by evidence, and would have been quite contrary to Egyptian royal practice.

Prince Amenhotep probably acceded to the throne about 1368 B.C., and took the names Neferkheprure Waenre Amenhotep, that is, he became Amenophis IV. Within two or three years however he had changed his last name to Akhenaten and adopted the worship of Aten. At the beginning of his reign he presumably resided mainly at Thebes; there he built very large temple buildings to the Aten in the precincts of the Karnak temple of Amen-Re. As these buildings were completely dismantled after Akhenaten's death and the blocks of which they were composed were used to fill pylons, it is uncertain whether Akhenaten attempted to convert the whole existing temple to the worship of the Aten, or whether he simply added shrines to the Aten to it. The work however shows the royal family worshipping the Aten disk, in the new, informal style adopted for official art at Amarna. Several famous tombs at Thebes belonging to officials of his father also received additions carved in this style.

In the sixth year of his reign, Akhenaten beat the bounds of his chosen new capital city, and ordered the carving of the great rock-stelae that mark its confines. These include not only the city on the east bank but a large area of agricultural terrain on the west bank opposite. The stela proclamation runs: "As my father the Aten lives, I will make Akhetaten for the Aten my father in this place. I will not make him Akhetaten south of it, north of it, west of it or east of it. And Akhetaten extends from the southern stela as far as the northern stela, measured between stela and stela on the eastern mountain, likewise from the south-west stela to the north-west stela on the western mountain of Akhetaten. And the area within these four stelae is Akhetaten itself; it belongs to Aten my father; mountains, deserts, meadows, islands, high ground and low ground, land, water, villages, men, beasts and all things which the Aten my father shall bring into existence eternally forever. I will not neglect this oath which I have made to the Aten my father eternally for ever." He visited Amarna again in year 8, while the city was being built, and added to the stelae; it would seem that it was in year 8 that Akhenaten, Nefertiti and their daughters finally installed themselves at Amarna. A passage in the boundary stelae has been interpreted to mean that Akhenaten swore never to leave his city, but this more probably refers to his not extending the boundaries of the city itself.

The whole interpretation of the events of these early years of Akhenaten's reign depends upon whether Amenophis III was still alive in year 9 of Akhenaten or whether he had died before Akhenaten acceded. Akhenaten endowed the Aten with a royal titulary, which he slightly changed in or about year 9. A number of inscriptions from Amarna and elsewhere have been shown to associate the royal names of Amenophis III and Akhenaten with the later form of the Aten titulary, and there exist scenes in which Amenophis III is shown, apparently alive, with the later Aten names. There are also various wine dockets and business documents which suggest, though they hardly prove, that year 1 of Akhenaten followed close upon year 27 of Amenophis III; yet the last year of Amenophis III was his 38th. Cumulatively therefore there is quite strong inferential evidence for assuming a coregency of from nine to twelve years between father and son. This would mean that all during the period of the foundation of Amarna and the early years of Akhenaten's residence there, Egypt was really being ruled by the senior King, Amenophis III, from Thebes. Amenophis III would thus have continued to rule a state of which the official cult was that of Amen-Re, while allowing his younger co-regent to build a new capital city for the cult of Aten and even to build monuments of the Aten at Karnak itself. This cannot be regarded as impossible, but conflicts oddly with what we know of the practice of the Pharaonic office; until a document dated by both kings is discovered which proves the long co-regency, it seems best to preserve an open mind. A letter from the King of Mitanni, Dušratta, which promises the same friendship to Akhenaten as he had observed with Akhenaten's dead father, Amenophis III, would settle the matter were the date of its docket fully preserved; but there is a lacuna before the extant figure 2, which means that the original may have read year 2 or year 12.

The life of the royal family at Amarna is most fully depicted in the reliefs on the walls of the rock tombs that the great state officials carved for themselves in the cliffs, though fascinating and delicate fragments of large frescoes from the royal palaces are also preserved. In the tombs the Pharaoh is shown with Nefertiti and his daughters in the Window of Appearances of the Royal Palace, bestowing honours and largesse on his bowing and obsequious high officials; again with his family, driving in his chariot between the temple of the Aten and the Palace along the Royal Way, escorted by his guard and applauded by the crowd; worshipping in the temple; or dining and drinking in the privacy of the palace. In all these scenes Nefertiti is shown as of equivalent stature to the King, and her names Neferneferuaten Nefertiti are enclosed in a cartouche; evidently she enjoyed the same influence at court as her predecessor Ty. Even in official scenes, the King and Queen are shown hand in hand; the scenes of them banqueting in the palaces are depicted with a wealth of intimate detail not normally recorded in Egyptian art.

The royal pair had six daughters, Meritaten, Maketaten, Ankhesenpaaten, Neferneferuaten the younger, Neferneferure and Setepenre, all of whom were born before year 9. Famous scenes in the tomb of Huy, the Chief Steward of the Royal Household of Queen Ty, record a visit of Queen Ty to Amarna some time before year 12 with her daughter Baketaten. A lintel in the tomb represents Amenophis III with Ty and Baketaten on one side, and Akhenaten, Nefertiti and four daughters on the other; some supporters of the co-regency believe this shows that Amenophis III himself visited Amarna very near to the end of his reign. A jubilee held for the King and the Aten in year 12, and a festival in which foreign tribute was ceremonially offered at a specially erected pavilion in the same year, mark for some scholars the beginning of Akhenaten's sole rule.

In all the scenes showing the King and his family, the disk of the sun is shown above them, extending its rays towards them; these rays end in hands, which sometimes hold the Egyptian symbol of life to the noses of the King and Queen. This favour is granted to them alone; where officials are shown in the doorways of their tombs reciting the famous hymns to the Aten, the god itself is not portrayed. Alone among Egyptian gods the Aten is given a royal titulary and celebrates periodical jubilees; significantly these are concurrent with the jubilees of the King. It is the King and Queen who are the chief actors in the cult of the Aten; their colossal statues surrounded the open courts of the temples, which apparently contained no images of the gods, although the walls were probably covered with scenes of the worship of Aten. The god was physically present in his disk above, and the cult seems mainly to have consisted in dedicating offering-libations, incense and oblations to open altars. The Aten communicated directly to the King, and it was the King alone who interpreted the divine will. In the longer hymn to the Aten, which has been thought to have been composed by the King himself, a long poetic passage ascribes the creation of all the phenomena of the universe to the Aten, and asserts that all creatures move and have their being only by virtue of the sun's rising and infusing life into them each morning. The final section runs:—

"Thou art in my heart, there is none that knows thee but thy son Neferkheperure Waenre, and thou hast made him wise through thy plans and thy omnipotence. The world exists by thy hand, as thou hast made them. When thou arisest, they live; when thou settest, they die. Thou art thyself the span of life, by thee do men live. Eyes can see beauty until thou settest; but when thou settest on the right all work is set aside. When thou risest, thou makest (all things?) to prosper for the King; (the power) of motion is in every leg (only) because thou hast founded the earth. Thou hast raised them up for thy son, who came forth from thy flesh, the King of Upper and Lower Egypt, who lives in Truth, the Lord of the Two Lands, Neferkheperure Waenre, the Son of the Re who lives in Truth, Lord of Diadems, Akhenaten, may he live long, and for the Great Royal Wife, his beloved, the Mistress of the Two Lands, Neferneferuaten Nefertiti, may she live and grow young for ever and ever."

While this hymn is certainly monotheistic in the sense that all creation and all power is ascribed exclusively to one sole being, yet the theocratic element is clear; the Aten rules only through his son Pharaoh Akhenaten, who is almost in the situation of the god's incarnation on earth. In this light it is not difficult to picture the motives for Akhenaten's persecution of all other gods in the later years of his reign.

After year 12, Queen Nefertiti disappears from the records. A number of objects inscribed with her name were found in a palace in the North City at Amarna; some have thought that she may have been disgraced and incarcerated there, but the evidence is very inadequate. She may well have died. At some point in time after this, probably in year 14, Akhenaten adopted as co-regent Smenkhkare, who was married to Akhenaten's eldest daughter Meritaten, presumably in order to affirm his claim to the throne in traditional XVIIIth Dynasty manner. Who Smenkhkare was is uncertain; perhaps he

THE SITE

The stelae set in the cliffs by Akhenaten in years 6-8 define the area of the city of Akhetaten on the east bank of the Nile and its agricultural territory on the west. The eastern cliffs enclose a bay of flat desert six miles long from north to south and three miles deep. From the bay a large desert *wadi* leads through the eastern hills: up a side *wadi* four miles from its entrance is the ruined royal tomb. Either side of this *wadi* in the cliffs are two groups of rock tombs excavated for the nobles of Akhenaten's court. Some of these were unfinished at the time the city was abandoned, and it is not certain that any received the burial for which it was intended, as they were deliberately ruined. But the reliefs of these tombs, splendidly recorded by N. de G. Davies

Plate A

A. Tell el-Amarna.

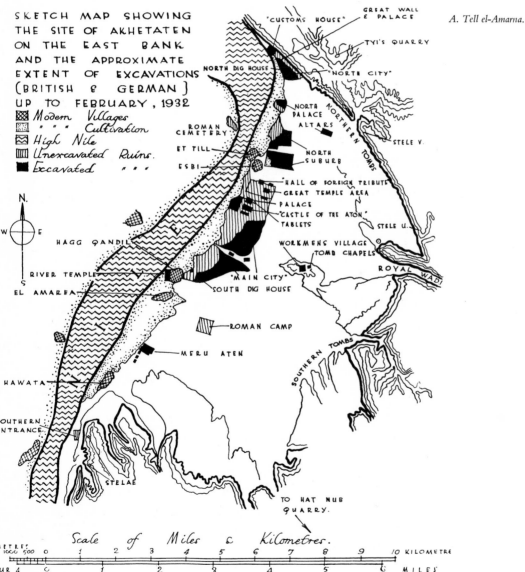

early in this century, are our chief source for the reconstruction of the appearance of the city of Akhetaten, and the life which Akhenaten and his court led there. These scenes are all in the new artistic style favoured by Akhenaten, which discards the formality of traditional Egyptian official art; they have one special value, namely that they contain detailed depictions of many of the buildings of the city. Though these are often difficult to interpret because of the Egyptian technique of combining plans and sections, and because the official buildings of the city have been razed in most cases to their foundations, yet many have been identified and their value may be assessed from the splendid reconstructions of the city published by the Egypt Exploration Society expedition.

B. Plan of the Central City.

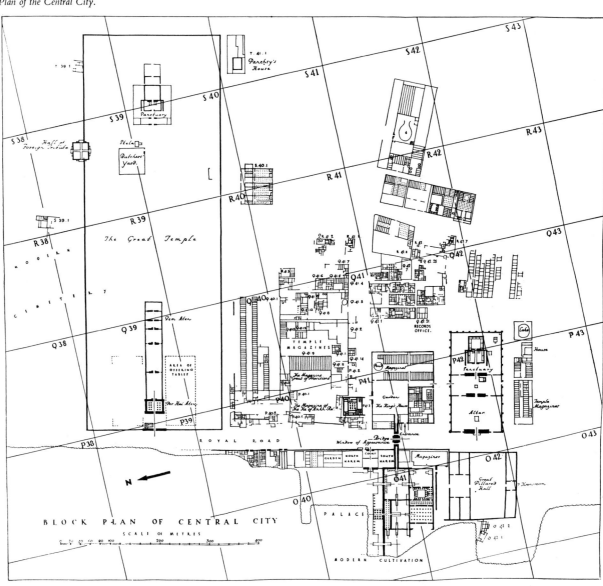

BLOCK PLAN OF CENTRAL CITY

SCALE OF METRES

Plan Plate B

Plate C. Lower, right corner

The city itself did not fill the whole bay, but lay along the river. Its nucleus, the "Central City", comprised the main public buildings and was probably built first. The river quays appear to have opened directly on to the "Great Palace", which comprises three separate constructions. The first, the "State Apartments", is a stone building of vast proportions, partly lost under the cultivation. Probably it was entered from the north through a gateway leading on to a huge court surrounded with colossal statues of the King and Queen. A pillared portico on the south led into a transverse pillared

10

hall and thence to a rectangular court. Beyond lay a series of three logitudinal pillared halls, which may have been throne rooms or audience chambers; they were flanked by colonnaded courts. Though it is clear that this building must have been used for the most impressive state ceremonies at Akhetaten, its exact status is unclear, as its plan is unique and few of its features have been identified in tomb representations. Beyond the audience chambers on the south lay an enormous hall built of mud brick with a forest of square pillars: this was evidently built hastily and rapidly rather late in the history of the city, and may have been Smenkhkare's coronation hall. The third element of

C. Reconstruction of the centre of the city.

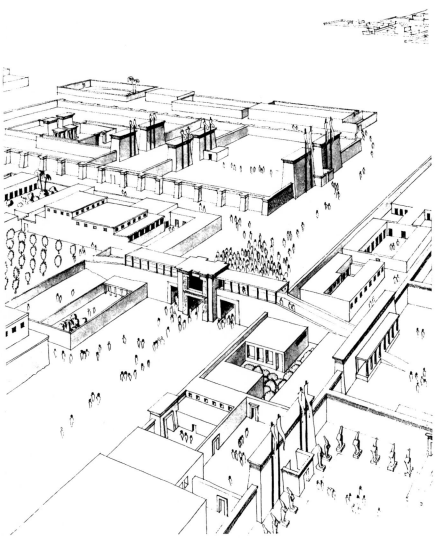

the "Great Palace" consists of the Royal Harem, the servants' quarters and magazines. These lie in a long narrow range of mud-brick buildings to the east of the state apartments along the length of the "Royal Road", Akhetaten's chief thoroughfare. The harems contained columned halls and courts, their pavements and walls delightfully painted and tiled with scenes of pools, plants, birds, fish and animal life; decorative rectangular pools were surrounded by loggias and private chambers.

A main ceremonial way led from the river through the internal courts

Plate C. Centre

11

of the State Apartments and the harems to a three-arched bridge over the Royal Road into the "King's House", where Akhenaten, Nefertiti and their daughters lived their private family life. It was probably on the bridge that the King's main "Window of Appearances" was situated: here there would have been a splendid view along this wide processional avenue and room for the crowds witnessing royal ceremonies. The "King's House" was not dissimilar in plan from the normal high official's villa, but was grander, and was surrounded by a spacious garden. On the south of the "King's House" was his private Temple to the Aten. Behind the "King's House" was the "Records Office", where in 1887 the cuneiform diplomatic archive known as the "Amarna Letters" was found. To the east again were quarters for the entertainment of foreign embassies and notabilities, and beyond on the desert edge, the barracks of the military and police.

Plate C. Left

Plate C. At the top

From the "King's House" it was a chariot ride of less than a quarter of a mile northwards along the "Royal Road" to the "Great Temple of the Aten", past large ranges of temple magazines. The temple enclosure forms a great rectangle on an east-west axis, entered through a pylon from the "Royal Road". A second pylon gave access to a hypostyle hall, called "The House of Rejoicing of the Aten". Along a processional way punctuated by gateways lay a series of six rectangular courts, called the "Gem-Aten", also filled with offering tables for oblations to the Sun's Disk. The central part of the enclosure was empty, but at its eastern end lay a sanctuary consisting of a pylon with porticoes and beyond a series of courts containing a great altar and offering tables. The pavilion where foreign tribute was received in year 12 lay abreast of the northern enclosure wall, while the high priest Panehsy's house lay outside the south-east corner of the enclosure.

To the south and north of the central buildings lay the main living areas of the city. The high officers of the Court evidently had the first choice of sites at Amarna, and in general sited their villas near to the Central City, in the main on the axis of the royal road. These villas consist basically of a courtyard, garden, garden shrine, porch, one or two open loggias, a main columnar entertaining room, a private hall, master bedroom, lavatory, bathroom, harem and extra bedrooms: a stairway led to the roof, while in the courtyard at the back were grain storage bins, ovens and other service facilities. Gaily painted decoration was often present in the main hall. Round these large villas, there congregated the houses of all the retainers of the great official, often built *pêle-mêle* and in haste regardless of the axes of the streets. The houses of the middle class in general formed orderly blocks in the South City and the North Suburb, where the quarter nearest the Aten Temple was occupied by corn merchants. The "Royal Road" progressed through the North Suburb to the North Palace, apparently a place of diversion, beautifully decorated, with fish ponds, aviaries and decorated mangers for several species of mammals. Beyond was the North City, surrounded by a great brick fortification wall, over the gate to which was probably another "Window of Appearances". Within was another large palace, which on rather fragile evidence has been considered to have been assigned to Queen Nefertiti after her alleged disgrace. Round this palace were great houses, which however had no dometic quarters, and may therefore have served as the official residences of the Vizier, Treasurer and other great dignitaries of state. At the extreme north end of the bay was a substantial building, perhaps a customs house, while at the southern end, separated from the city, was a royal pleasure pavilion known as the Maruaten. Industrial sites were scattered, but on the whole, like the glass works and sculptors' workshops were not far from the "Great Palace".

Such was the city of Akhetaten. Hastily built and casually planned parts of it certainly were: yet as the restorations in the Egypt Exploration Society's reports vividly demonstrate, its central quarters were of great dignity and architectural harmony. As the material described in this work shows, this was matched by decorative ingenuity, delicacy and taste: the effect on any embassy arriving from a foreign land must have been one of overwhelming beauty. Owing to the hazards of excavation in the Nile Valley, Tell el-Amarna is the only great ancient Egyptian city of which any major proportion has been dug; and this may well remain so. It is also the only city from which all the finds can be exactly dated to a short period of twenty years. Publication of evidence upon which its evaluation depends is therefore vital, and Mrs. Samson's book is devoted to this end.

The Significance of the Collection
by the author

Perhaps the significance of this Collection from Amarna was best discerned by Jean Capart, the eminent Belgian egyptologist, who described it to me as the greatest teaching collection in the world. The clue to this achievement can be found in Petrie's own words from the site where, in his day-to-day Journal he wrote of the glass he was finding "I keep every scrap to show the colours and patterns of this age". This approach of his led to the formation of a collection within which it is possible again and again to find the parallel or cite the example needed to make a point in the explanation of the Amarna civilisation. In it there is evidence on some of the questions which have puzzled egyptologists and the material covers a wide field of information about Akhenaten's city, Akhetaten, now called Amarna. The great majority of the objects are from Petrie's excavation of the central city in 1891-92, particularly in and around the Great Palace and the Great Temple, and further south. This gives a homogeneity to the finds, and where a piece can be assigned to a part of one of these vast edifices it can indicate developments which occurred as the building progressed. Other objects were bought by Petrie; some have been acquired direct from the excavations on the site by the Egypt Exploration Society between the years 1921-1937, and others from these digs came with the gift to the Museum from the Wellcome Trustees in 1964.

Chronologically the Collection spans the whole of the Amarna period, from the scarab on which Akhenaten is still named Amenophis (IV), to the stela where he is shown as co-regent with his son-in-law Smenkhkare. Historically it includes the sealing stamp which is very possibly a relic of Queen Ty's visit to Amarna in year 12, as well as the little gold figure from Qurneh that indicates the presence of the youngest Amarna princesses at the Court of Tutankhamen when he returned to Thebes.

Plates 55b, 55c

The fragments of the stela are published in their present form for the first time. They have been pieced together over the years since as a student of Professor Glanville, I began finding them in the Museum and interpreting them. It was then that I visited the Egypt Exploration Society's dig at Amarna, directed by J. D. S. Pendlebury, and he asked me to include some objects from this Collection with his finds from the site in "City of Akhenaten III". This led to Professor Fairman discerning that a fragment of limestone in Cairo found by Pendlebury in 1934 belonged to the Petrie Stela. Since then more fragments have been joined together.

Plate 5a

There are objects in the Collection that record the passing of the years in the city of Akhetaten. In the trio, the young Akhenaten and Nefertiti with, probably, their eldest daughter and heiress Meritaten as a child, are shown as

14

a normal family, not as the stylised impersonal royalty of the past. The Queen wears the typical Theban wig and not, as in the later pair statue of the King and Queen in the Louvre, her tall crown by which the world now knows her. Plate 5b The carving of the apron on the King's *shendyt* kilt is unfinished and by comparisons, explains the unfinished state of the King's one nude colossal statue from Karnak about which for years there has been so much supposition, including the theory that he was not able to father his six daughters. In these statuettes he is shown without the exaggeration that occurred when the art form changed from the monumental Egyptian style to expressionism.

On a fragment of diorite a young princess is shown with the gross caricaturing of that early period. She has the ovoid head with which the princesses Plate 26 are shown when young, although the old theory that all six had deformed heads is no longer credible. Some probably shared the family dolicocephalic skull, but as adults they are shown normally like Ankhesenamen is on Tutan- Plates 14b, 42 khamen's furniture. On a band from a column in the central palace which, on Plate 27 architectural and stylistic grounds can be judged as later than the diorite relief, the softening of the lines in the princess's portrait can be seen.

This mellowing of the art is evident too, in the contrasts between Nefertiti's portraits from the early years when the city was being built and Plate 18 the sketch of her in her later years wearing the tall crown. Akhenaten's Plate 19 profile, although only partial, also records the move towards naturalism. Plate 23 The small, unfinished head of Nefertiti in the round immortalises a stage in Plates I, 2 the carving of a masterpiece and is remarkable in its likeness to the painted Plate 3 limestone head in Berlin and the unfinished example. Plate 4

Innovations are visible in the scenes of daily life at Amarna. The relief of two offering bearers enables comparison between the way ordinary people Plate 28 are presented at Amarna and in similar scenes from the preceding reign in Thebes. In place of the exquisitely carved, elegant, stiffly posed stock figures of a procession in the tomb of Ramose, these two young temple attendants are individuals. Forging ahead as they do in eager movement with their offerings, the relief is an example of the use of space in a composition and the use of angles to urge a design forward. The second figure, slightly smaller, which gives a degree of perspective to the design, is carrying a stack of bouquet "cones" about the use of which queries have been expressed. When compared with those on the raised border of the stela on plate 55a, it seems likely that these are flower holders for an upright stand.

The unfinished figure from the tomb of Ay records the participation of a Plate 29 humble onlooker in an Amarna scene, apart from being a lamentable reminder of the thieving of works of art from the site in the last century. In the painted relief of the food carrier another vitalising Amarna influence is evident in the way the design breaks through the rigid lines of the registers to enliven a scene; and vitality is not limited to the larger and more important works in the city. It is evident on the ring bezels and seals where foreign Plate 46 parallels, which became a factor in the Empire of the XVIIIth Dynasty, are Plate 48 noticeable. The movements of animals in this small art echoes the love of nature expressed on the wall and floor painting in the palaces.

From the thousands of pieces of glazed and inlaid tiles which Petrie brought back, with hundreds of the moulds in which they were made, the faience industry can be seen as an integral part of Amarna art and architecture.

It must have assumed almost the proportions of the building itself, for the remains of glazed decorations abound, from walls, doors, columns, and possibly floors, from composite statues, composite inlaid portraits on the walls, inlays on the furniture and from inscriptions, besides the multiplicity of the faience small art that was worn and used in daily life. The varied fragments from the central city are proof of the intricacy of detail lavished on the faience objects of which but a small selection are included in this book.

The colour sense of the designers is shown in such examples as the red tiles inlaid with green leaves, white and yellow lotuses and buds, forming garlands against a red ground. The sophisticated use of colour perspective is evident in the warm colour over a colder hue on the tile of a duck which must be one of the earliest examples of such finesse in the art history of the world. The recognition of the effectiveness of mosaic patterns can also be seen in faience examples.

Faience inlays in the Collection include squares, circles, rhomboids, all the geometric shapes which studded the capitals of the palm-shaped columns in the palace. There are curved, glazed "ropes" from cartouches, rods from the Aten's rays and pieces of red and blue glazed disks of the Aten which Petrie notes were as large as fifteen centimetres in diameter. Fruits, flowers, fish and lotuses from pond scenes and marsh reeds from around them; foreigners, figures of gods and offerings for the Aten, all spell the variety of the inlaid scenes. If these splendours, like the fragments of faience vases and vessels, jewellery, bowls and kohl tubes with royal names on them, which Petrie found around the palace, were confined to it and the larger houses, the faience *minutiae* were not, since the beads and amulets were found by Woolley as far afield as the houses of the workmen in their Eastern Desert Village and must have been for the whole population. These merit a book to themselves. The numerous and varied amulets are a record of the degree of inspiration and courage of Akhenaten's endeavour to establish a universal monotheism at this period of world history, and, in a country so entrenched in the worship and fear of hundreds of animal and anthropomorphic gods and goddesses. They also record the freedom allowed in the city built and dedicated to the sole worship of the Aten. Amongst the amulets are also some of the Aten symbols.

There is ample evidence in the Collection of the multiplicity of scenes dedicated to the Aten. Some reliefs evince the religious emphasis and the stimulated understanding of the artists in their purpose of expressing the King's beliefs. The sculptors were faced on unprecedented scale with the challenge of carving scenes of religious and royal significance to be seen in the direct light of the sun. The Aten ceremonies on the walls and stelae of the roofless temples and courts had to convey their message at all times of the day, at different heights and with the changing emphasis from cast shadows. How successfully the challenge was met could only be known if any of the carvings in the city had remained *in situ*. The evidence of the way the sculptors worked is clear from many pieces in the Collection. They varied the cutting angles and the depth of line and combined the different techniques of sunk-relief (*en creux*) and raised reliefs (*en bas*) in the one subject, sometimes supplementing the emphasis with colour, according to the material and methods used. Two relevant examples are the libation offerings,

Plates VI, VIII

Plate VII

Plate VI

Plates 24, 25

16

where the variation would focus the attention of the viewer on the devotional activity in all angles of light from the sun. Similarly, the Queen's profile on the alabaster balustrade which, leading to one of the raised doors in the palace would largely be seen above the heads of the people on floor level, is in the same genre as her portrait on the marble fragment, but the two carvings are given different emphasis of line and depth.

The understanding of a third dimension is evident in the placing of Aten rays behind a head and, in the relief of the offering bearers, by size as mentioned above, as well as by placing the bouquet behind the head of the man on the left. Some of the stone inlay portraits show the same awareness and at least one has rounded edge carving, to remain above the surface of the wall and cast a shadow. Others are intended to be sunk into the wall flush with the surface. In the best of these the planes of the face are carved so that a play of light would achieve what a tonal painter does by varying hue and tone. The carving of the head of a negro for inlay is bolder but not without modelling on the face; it shows the non-royal inlay, without preparation for the addition of features and regalia which created the composite royal inlays in the style of composite statues. There are pieces of varying sizes in the Collection from such composite statues, the finest being the superbly carved life sized red jasper ankle and heel which would have been joined at the top surface by the gown of the wearer, possibly in limestone or alabaster, just as the king and queen's robes drop to their ankles on the back of Tutankhamen's golden throne. Besides carvings of part of a face in this red jasper, there are other pieces from composite statues including a heavy carving of part of a full sized wig in basalt, curved pieces of blue faience from the King's war crown and a small faience slightly curved crown of Nefertiti's, probably from a statuette.

The naturalistic female statuettes found in the palace and central city would seem to be from groups of the Queen and her daughters. They echo the form of the earlier statues of the King and Queen with their oldest daughters at the base of some of the Boundary Stelae and more information would undoubtedly be obtained if all the examples of these so called "princess" figures, in widely scattered museums, could be considered together. The apparently careless placing of a right hand on the left side of the sandstone "princess" figure is a very unusual example of a pre-Homeric nod amongst the Amarna sculptors of statues, although in reliefs even royal figures are sometimes given two left or right hands. There is an instance of this occurring on the owner of the stela, despite the rigorous training evident in the studies of hands.

The technically high level reached by the stone carvers can be seen in detail in such signs from inscriptions.[*] Even on the stamps for clay sealings with the inscriptions of many horses and Queen Ty's name, the carving is competent and would have produced a bold design in the clay, in *bas relief*, as on the first and outermost door of Tutankhamen's tomb. This detailed skill is particularly evident in the carving of the stone inlays where, against the smooth surface the masons gave the fine white limestone, the multi-coloured red and black granite and diorite inscriptions were inlaid and must have been visible, even legible from a distance. Cornices of black granite uraei were inlaid in yellow quartzite, white alabaster was inlaid in red granite,

Plate 20

Plate 18

Plate 24
Plate 28

Plate 38

Plate 40

Plate 41

Plate II

Plate 14b
UC 112
UC 076
UC 24274
UC 24270

Plates 8a-11

Plate 10

Plate 55
Plate 35

*Plates 36, 44 and 53

Plate 44

17

and other combinations used. The competence in carving the brittle stones is consummate. In the smaller inscriptions glass was used for the slim lines of which one limestone piece in the Collection is a fine example.

The glass makers were also artists. The unique fragment of the two young princesses, early in the history of moulded glass, shows most of the techniques of their craft and at the same time, the artistry of the pose portrays their youthfulness. Another fine example is the head for inlay, possibly another portrait of a princess. Nothing remains of the delicate inlaid furniture from Amarna which must be imagined from pieces like these. Only on Tutankhamen's furniture is there the possibility of a parallel. The frail gold figure from Qurneh, probably an Amarna princess living at his Court, is possibly from something belonging to him.

No pottery is included in this book and it is anticipated that a study of Mycenaean sherds from Amarna will be published later.

Life at Amarna was cultivated; the philosophy advanced for its time; the state unwarlike; the daily life dedicated; nature was appreciated and humour evident. It was a background against which artists could, and did develop. Two unofficial masterpieces in the Collection which testify to their enjoyment are the alabaster "swimming" girl from the perfume holder, and the sketch of a baboon, possibly brushed in on the limestone during an idle moment, and remaining as a tribute to the mastery of the Ancient Egyptian draughtsman.

UC 190

Plate V

Plate 45

Plates 42, 43 and IV

Plates 12a and 12b
Plate 37

Statues and Statuettes

HEAD OF AKHENATEN

This ushabti head of Akhenaten from his tomb was bought by Petrie and exhibited in London on his return from Amarna in 1892. Wearing the *Khat* or "bag" wig with the pigtail at the back, and the uraeus and beard, it resembles a number of other ushabtis from the tomb, particularly one in Brooklyn.[1] But the finely boned features have an unusual delicacy and are strikingly like those of Queen Ty in the schist head from Sinai.[2] The face also resembles Tutankhamen in his statue as Khonsu from Karnak,[3] and his portrait in the Theban trio with Amen and Mut.[4] The eyebrows, nose and full, slightly drooping lips are clearly defined, but the eyes are suggested in a way that gives the face the dreaminess of a contemplative, evident in other remarkable portraits of the King.

[UC 007]
Provenance: Amarna, Royal Tomb. Syenite. Height 7·0 cm. Width 6·0 cm. Lit. W. M. F. Petrie, *Catalogue of Antiquities from Amarna*, 1892, p. 5. J. Samson, *C/A III*, Text, p. 225, pl. CV(12). Comparisons: [1]Brooklyn, No. 33.53(3); [2]Cairo 38257; [3]Cairo 38488; [4]G. Legrain, C.C.G., I, pl. LXII, No. 42.097.

1. Head of Akhenaten showing family resemblance to Tutankhamen. (H. 7 cm.).

HEAD OF NEFERTITI

The arresting similarity of this small unfinished head to the famous painted limestone head of the Queen in Berlin,[1] and to the lesser known unfinished head also found by the Germans in the studio of the sculptor Thutmose,[2] points to the same provenance for this carving, perhaps even the same master hand for it also bears the mark of genius. It has already been given the meditative repose of Amarna royal portraits described by M. Vandier as *"le mystère d'une vie intérieure intense"*.

The poise of the Queen's head on her long neck is characteristic. Her distinctive cheekline is suggested, her long eyelid and the straight nose. Her full sensuous mouth, so sharply defined in the Berlin portraits is beginning to be shaped and when finished would have completed the profile of her mature years. On her head is the roughly hewn peg for the addition of her upright crown in another material. The shaping of the ear and the treatment of the stone are at an earlier stage than on the unfinished Berlin portrait.

[UC 010]
Provenance: Amarna (possibly studio of Thutmose). Red sandstone. Height 6·5 cm. Width 6·0 cm. Lit. J. Samson, *C/A III*, text p. 225, pl. *CV* (11). Comparisons: [1]*Cat. Ägyptisches Museum*, Berlin, Inv. No. 21300; [2]*M.D.O.G.* 52, pl. 5.

2. Head of Nefertiti with preparation for tall crown to be added in another material. (H. 6·5 cm.).

Facsimile of Colour Plate I. See p. 64.

3. Unfinished Head of Nefertiti (Berlin).
(H. 36 cm.).

4. Painted limestone head of Nefertiti
(Berlin). (H. 50 cm.).

ROYAL TRIO

The unfinished limestone statuette of Akhenaten, Nefertiti and a young princess is important as a record of the early period at Amarna, and for the comparison it affords with other carvings and later developments.

The small triad is cut from a single block of limestone. The King and Queen, backed by a plinth, step forward on a rectangular platform base, while the princess lags childlike on the right of her mother. Her head and the top of the Queen's wig were freed from the plinth which apparently continued behind the taller head of the King, presumably planned to wear a crown.

His clavicles are carved with undue prominence considering his fleshy torso and thighs, with the disproportion evident in early Amarna attempts to show the royal figures realistically. But his figure here, fleshy like his father's in his later years when the artistic realism began, is more that of an oriental monarch than a body distorted by disease. The apron of his *shendyt* kilt has been shaped, but the carving of the kilt not started and this unfinished work is useful for comparison as described below. The King's hand is missing from his left arm which hangs close to his side, while his right arm stretches towards the Queen as they clasp hands in the manner of their pair statue in the Louvre, discussed later,[1] and like the model hands found in Thutmose's studio.[2]

Nefertiti stands with her left foot forward like the King, in the active pose more usual in other periods for a man, rather than his wife. Both wear sandals. The Queen has the taut, upright body of a young woman and wears

[UC 004]
Provenance: A sculptor's studio near the south end of Amarna. Limestone. Height 13·5 cm. Width 11·0 cm. [1]Louvre No. E.15593; [2]M.D.O.G. No. 50, fig. 25; [3]M.D.O.G. No. 52, fig. 25; [4]Cairo, 55938; [5]Cairo, 49528. Lit. [6]P. *T/A.*, p. 31, Pl. I(1); [7]J. Capart, *Rec. de monuments égyptiens*, II, Pl. LXXV, Brussels, 1905.

the Theban wig, not her later Amarna variety, with the lappets hanging from it to her breasts. Between the lappets an oblique line is incised possibly marking the top edge of her gown. Below each breast is an echoing upward curving line, probably to be smoothed away eventually. Her navel is but a rounded depression, in contrast to the triangular shape with a line through it more usual in later years, and at the base of her abdomen are two upward curving lines. Her knees and legs are blocked in somewhat "woodenly".

5a. Royal trio—unfinished limestone statuette of Akhenaten, Nefertiti and a princess. (H. 13·5 cm.).

To the right of the Queen and turning slightly away is the small figure of a princess, possibly Meritaten, towards whom her mother holds out her right arm which swings behind her to catch the child's left hand. The left upper arm of the princess remains, stretching out along a ridge similar to that on Plate 8a* the left of the figure.* The princess has been given her mother's figure in miniature in the manner used by the artists during the early years of the new art when the children are merely small adults, but there is no suggestion of clothing as on her parents, so she may have been planned to remain naked and shoeless in the informal manner sometimes used for the young princesses at Amarna. Her left foot is forward in the emancipated pose. Her right arm, now missing, appears to have hung down close beside her body. The statuette is without an inscription.

22

For similarities and contrasts, the group is useful to compare with the later limestone dyad of the King and Queen in the Louvre. This is on the same scale, but finished, painted and inscribed. In both statuettes, the royal figures are hand-in-hand and stepping forward on a shallow platform base away from a back plinth. In the Louvre pair, Akhenaten, wearing the blue crown, steps forward with a resolute air; Nefertiti is wearing the tall crown introduced during the Amarna years, and her figure has the suggestion of the droop which is more pronounced in the ageing figure of her standing statuette from the Thutmose studio.[3] The Aten names on the back of the Louvre plinth are in the late form prevalent after year 9, and the couple are unattended by a princess, the eldest of whom by then would have been entering her teens.

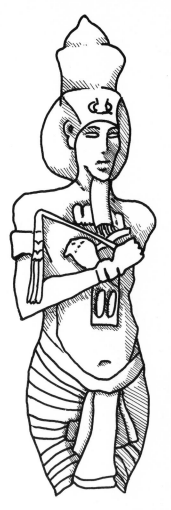

6. Diagram of finished colossus of Akhenaten (Cairo).

5b. Akhenaten and Nefertiti (Louvre). (H. 23 cm.).

On the dyad, the apron of the King's *shendyt* kilt is carved as it has been started in the trio, and comparison shows the actual method used for carving the kilt, which settles the long controversy as to how it could have been added to the King's nude statue from Karnak. The belt is made by cutting back the surface of the abdomen to leave a ridge, and the linen folds of the kilt are then carved over the hips, curving up to the belt buckle. On the one unfinished colossal statue of Akhenaten found in Karnak, the only one that is nude[4], his kilt would have been added in this way, because the stone is already recessed around the Aten plaques at the waist and would have been further cut back, as on the finished colossus, to make the ridge of the belt.[5] There would have been no necessity for further delineation of the King's figure, about which there has been so much conjecture, any more than on the two

7. Diagram of unfinished colossus of Akhenaten (Cairo).

23

statuettes. This underlines the fallibility of theories about his physical build and condition being based on unfinished statues. Rather than the son of the sun choosing to be represented as unable to father his children, the probability is that the one nude, unfinished statue was never raised to a standing position. It is unlikely that the Amen priests left in Thebes after the royal removal to Akhetaten would have exerted every effort to finish the Aten temple, and if Nefertiti's daughters were the children of someone else and not Akhenaten, it is inexplicable why a son was not introduced into the royal household as an heir.

Petrie found the trio at a "sculptor's place . . . near the south end of the town",[6] presumably Thutmose's. Both he and Capart[7] thought it may have been a model for larger works, possibly like those beneath the Boundary Stelae to which it has resemblances as described on page 28, but it may have been intended as a finished, coloured limestone statuette like the Louvre dyad.

As it stands, it is a record of the royal family, possibly soon after their arrival at Amarna, with the Queen's youthful figure and Theban styled wig, the child princess, and her parents in a protective normal rôle.

NEFERTITI OR A 'PRINCESS' FIGURE

Although known as "The Amarna Princess" for well over half a century, recent comparisons of it with other "princess" figures discovered since its acquisition, and with figures of Nefertiti, suggest that this is not a figure of a princess but a portrait of the Queen.

Plate 8a

In reddish brown quartzite, the upright torso stands gracefully against a plinth. The body is rounded to behind the hips and on the left of the figure was another feature, now grossly destroyed. The head, which was evidently carved in one piece with the body, is broken from the base of the neck, of which the roughened horizontal circle remains. In front of this is the lower edge of the clavicles. Both legs are missing from above the knees, but the right thigh is carved in advance from a stance of one foot forward. The carving of the front of the torso is unspoilt and the figure has a flesh-like reality from the fine burnish of the stone. The smoothed surface of the upright shoulders continues over to the top of the broken back plinth. The breasts are youthfully small and firm in contrast to the abdomen and full hips which are those of a *multiperae* rather than a young girl. There is a horizontal line through the navel as on other examples of such nude torsos from Amarna and on the draped figure in the Louvre, thought to be the Queen.[1]

The broken surface of the back plinth on which no trace of burnish or inscription remains, now slopes obliquely down from the shoulders, and outwards to whatever feature stood at the far end of the ridge, left of the figure. The left arm swings back to meet this at hand level, probably to reach a small following princess whose arm stretched forward along the slightly downward slope of the ridge to meet her mother's hand. The once rounded arm of the main figure is chipped on the top surface, but still finely burnished at the back, as the stone is above and below the ridge.

24

8a. Nefertiti or a princess figure with left arm swung back like the Queen's right arm in the trio plate 5a. (H. 15·3 cm.).

[UC 002]
Provenance: Amarna. Reddish quartzite. Height 15·3 cm. Width 8·0 cm.
Width at top of broken back plinth
5·5 cm.; at bottom 7·5 cm. Width of
chiselled surface right of the figure at
thigh level: 8·0 cm. Comparisons:
[1]Louvre, W.25409, C. Desroches-
Noblecourt, *L'Ancienne Égypte*,
*L'Extraordinaire Aventure Armén-
ienne*, Paris, 1960. [2]Ashmolean
Museum, Oxford, 1893-1-41 (260);

*8b. Side view showing ridge as from
princess's arm on plate 5a. (H. 15·3 cm.).*

Plate 9

The right arm of the figure is missing. It was freed from the stone at the
elbow and the forearm could have reached forward to meet the hand of
another in a group. Below the roughened surface where the upper arm was
joined, the stone is finely burnished. But although the surface at right angles
to this is squared, it is roughly finished with the chisel marks remaining,
unlike the other surfaces of the block and as though planned to flank
another figure or object.

This links the figure with a named one of the Queen in Oxford[2] and
differentiates them both from so-called "princess" figures, some of which have
the remains of a princess's name or title. A number of these were also clearly
part of a group and all are headless with the legs mostly broken near the
knees or at the top. In most it can be seen that one leg was in advance of the
other; in a number one arm hung down by the side and in some one arm is
bent across the body at the waist, but these poses of the legs and arms were
not always carved uniformly on the left or right side and appear as though
varied to balance the composition of the figures in a group. In contrast to
these poses the statuette described here resembles figures of the Queen with
one arm stretched towards a princess as in the trio above and in the treatment
of a Boundary Stela statue described below. The stone of the Oxford figure
of the Queen is savagely broken but is carved in the same way as these other
statuettes and, considered with the figure here, and "princess" figures, suggests
that a number of these came from more than one group of Nefertiti with
her daughters.

26

Comparison of these nude statuettes shows the use of and even probably the grouping of different stones in the Amarna tradition. Of the three in this Collection, two are quartzite and one sandstone. In Brooklyn, apart from a larger figure of Maketaten in quartzite,[3] there is one in granite found by Pendlebury in the Broad Hall of the central palace.[4] Another found by him in the same area is of sandstone;[5] two in San Diego are in sandstone, one of Meritaten, found by him in the palace,[6] and another with the fragmentary designation "born of";[7] one in Berlin is of sandstone.[8] The figure of Nefertiti in Oxford is of quartzite. Without seeing and handling all the above examples a full comparison is not possible.

Plates 8a, 10, and 11

The arguments in detail for the largest figure in this Collection being Nefertiti and not a princess are as follows:—

1 Like the Oxford figure of the Queen, this has one side squared but un-finished as though to stand beside another. Both these figures have been carved from quartzite with a dark streak running through it and in both this has been used down the right side of the figure to enhance its round-ness. Such attentive selection of the stone and skilled use of it suggests special care given in the same studio to portraits of the Queen.

[3]Brooklyn, 16.46; [4]J. D. S. Pendlebury, *C/A III*, No. 237, p. 67, pl. LXIX (2); [5]J. D. S. Pendlebury, *op. cit.*, No. 260, p. 68, pl. LXIX (2); [6]J. D. S. Pendlebury, *op. cit.*, No. 261, p. 68, pl. LXIX (2); [7]San Diego Museum, 15298; [8]H. Schäfer, ZÄS, 52, p. 82, pl. 17, Leipzig, 1915.

9. Part of figure of Nefertiti (Ashmolean Museum). (H. 121 cm.).

[9]N. de G. Davies, *RTA*, V, pl. XLI, XLIII. [10]J. Capart, *Lectures on Egyptian Art*, p. 26, fig. 19, University of North Carolina, 1928, and O.U.P. H. Schäfer, *Amarna in Religion und Kunst*, D.O.G. Berlin, pl. 23, 1931. Burlington Fine Arts Club, *Illustrated Cat. of Ancient Egyptian Art*, p. IX, 1930. J. F. Harris, *Egyptian Art*, Spring Books, pl. 28, London, 1936. J. Samson, *C/A III*, p. 226, pl. CVI. J. Vandier, *La Statuaire Égyptienne*, pl. CXI, (5), Paris, 1958.

2 The left arm of this figure swings back to meet the ridge like Nefertiti's arm in the trio above, where her hand clasps the hand of the following princess. This also echoes the technique used on the right side of the Queen's statue below Boundary Stela A where a ridge links the arm of the princess with her mother's figure.[9]

3 The right arm of this example was freed from the elbow and could have reached towards another as the Queen does to the King in the trio above and in other groups.

4 This figure has neither an arm crossing the body nor hanging by its side, both attributes of named figures of the princesses.

The hacking out of names and the almost uniform destruction of these statuettes across the thinner parts of the figures, while leaving the bulk of the stone as found in the palace, points to the aim of the damage being to obliterate the royal portrait rather than to plunder the stone. Had these figures been only of princesses, the attacks may have been less purposeful. If a figure of the King had been included in such groups, its handleable size would undoubtedly have resulted in its total destruction.

Over 40 years ago, Jean Capart, noting that Petrie bought this figure, wrote that he believed it may have come from the studio of Thutmose and he added that he had "hard work to convince one of the most celebrated classical archaeologists that this piece of work was dated seven centuries before the first efforts of the Greeks in statuary."[10]

It is hindsight and the knowledge of "princess" figures excavated since then that enables the present assessment of this as a portrait of the Queen, and not of an Amarna Princess as it has always been described in the past.

FRAGMENT OF A 'PRINCESS' FIGURE

[UC 24324] (W)
Provenance: Broad Hall, Central Palace, Amarna. Sandstone. Height 11·3 cm. Central front width 5·5 cm. Back width 7 cm. Length of arm and hand 5 cm. Lit. *C/A III*, excavation report, p. 66, No. 37, otherwise unpublished. Comparison pl. 55.

Although lacking the fine finish of the stonework on the more fully preserved quartzite torso this sandstone fragment is from a figure in the same *genre*. It was found by Pendlebury in the Broad Hall of the Central Palace at Amarna, with others discussed more generally above. The lower left side of the abdomen remains; the curve of the break left of its centre is made from the line across the navel which is usual in these figures. The pubic fullness is also a typical feature. Part of the upper left thigh remains and a fraction of the right leg showing it was advanced. Left of the figure is a hand and wrist, carved as though it were a right hand. The back of it rests against the thigh with thumb in front and palm and fingers outwards, not possible in a left hand nor in a position which the right hand of this figure could be. It could be the right hand of an adjacent figure, which would be unlike other examples of these group figures with this feature remaining; or it could be a hand carved in a reversed position, which although not unusual in Amarna reliefs where incorrectly placed hands occur in numerous places, is an unexpected carelessness in a carving in the round. Other examples on these figures are in the correct position. The hand rests against a piece of dressed stone, at right angles to the figure and sloping slightly backwards.

See, for example, Plate 55

28

The figure is broken in the middle from front to back nearly at a right angle to the front. The back is completely broken leaving a nearly flat broken surface.

10. Left thigh, and a hand on a "princess" figure. The fraction of right leg is shown slightly forward. (H. 11·3 cm.).

11. Fragment of "princess" figure with back plinth, similar to others from groups. (H. 11·3 cm.).

FRAGMENT OF A 'PRINCESS' FIGURE

This fragment of a nude torso from the original Petrie Collection is of red quartzite. It is broken almost horizontally across the middle and unevenly across the thighs, leaving from waist to thigh on the right side of the body and only the lower abdomen on its left. Although so fragmentary, it is comparable in style with other "princess" figures from Amarna, with the up-curving line in the pubic area. The navel is without the horizontal line through it that these figures usually show.

A protuberance of rough stone down the left side of the figure could have been its arm and hand. The buttocks are rounded and carved on both sides to meet a narrow projecting plinth at the centre back. Although once of dressed stone, the left side of the plinth is completely beaten away and the right side grossly damaged, but on this there are faint signs of shapes which might once have been parts of hieroglyphs.

[UC 082]
Provenance: Amarna. Red quartzite. Height 6·0 cm. Width 8·0 cm. Width of body across top break 6·0 cm. Width of plinth: 2·3 cm. Diameter 8·0 cm. Unpublished.

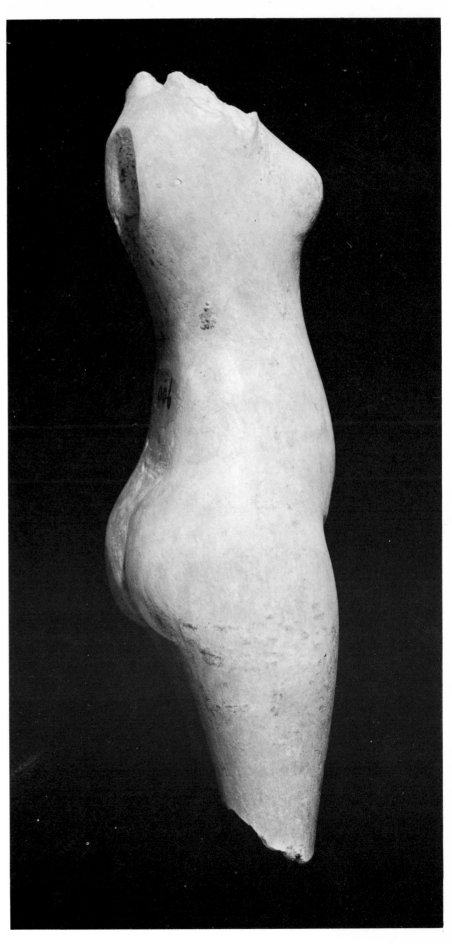

12a. "Swimming" girl with mortise between the shoulders for her head which would look towards the perfume container that would be held in her outstretched hands. (L. 8·3 cm.).

FIGURE FROM A PERFUME HOLDER

This young girl's figure is part of a toilet spoon of the familiar XVIIIth Dynasty shape where a girl lies prone with her head raised and her arms outstretched in front of her to hold a perfume container. There is a rounded mortise between her shoulders where her neck would have fitted, with her head carved to look forward to the perfume dish in her hands.

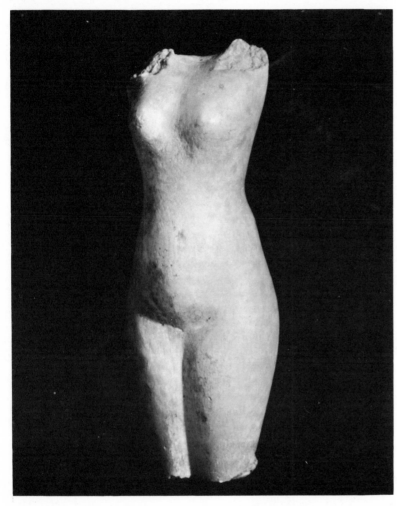

12b. Upright view of the alabaster figure which held a perfume or unguent container. (L. 8·3 cm.).

[UC006]
Provenance: Amarna. Alabaster. Length 8·5 cm. Width 3·5 cm. Lit. J. Samson, *C/A III*, p. 227, pl. CVI (2 and 6).

Despite the missing head, arms and lower legs, the shapely breasts and the flowing lines of her body suggest the flexibility of youth, and the curve of the back with the tautly stretched muscles each side of the waist give the pose a sense of action and show the artist's understanding of anatomy.

Sometimes described as "swimming girls" these figures were carved in wood and ivory as well as stone and although the craftsmanship is usually high, some are stylised and rigid. This figure has the sensitivity of a masterpiece, like the royal portraits of the later Amarna period.

BUST FROM A ROYAL STATUE

This quartzite bust from a half life-sized seated royal statue is carved in the finest tradition of the sculptor's technique in hard stone. It is from a composite statue, and the neck is mortised with a clear-cut central rectangle, 6·7 centimetres from front to back, to take the head.

31

[UC 001]
Provenance: Amarna. Red quartzite. Height 20·0 cm. Frontal width 17·0 cm. Width of left shoulder to centre back 10·0 cm. Lit. W. M. F. Petrie, *History of Egypt II*, p. 224, London, 1899. J. Samson, *C/A III*, p. 226, pl. CV (9). Comparison: W. C. Hayes, *Scepter of Egypt, II*, p. 285, fig. 173, N.Y., 1968.

13a. Front view of royal statue bust showing a mortise for the head, and wearing a collar-necklace with Aten plaques of which there are faience examples in the Collection. (H. 20 cm.).

The damage the bust has suffered appears to have been purposeful. Besides the loss of the right arm, the left is broken from above the elbow and the stone below the waist of the figure has apparently been beaten away. The right breast has been reduced by abrasion, and the left one flattened; this has removed part of the Aten plaques on the left of the necklace and the central pair above the waist. All the plaques contain the early name of the Aten; the top of a cartouche remains on the left arm.

13b. Side view of royal statue bust showing wrinkles above the waist suggesting a sitting pose. (H. 20 cm.).

The shapely body has wrinkles both sides above the waist, suggesting plumpness in a sitting figure, but the clavicles and the hollows between them are well defined and the back is curved between the *scapulae* into a slight hollow, where streamers as from a crown are incised. Pleats of the gown are carved over the left shoulder to fall downwards across the body into the long robe so often worn by Nefertiti and occasionally by Akhenaten. As in the similar limestone bust of the Queen in the Metropolitan Museum, New York, the robe is carved over the breast! The carving of the pleats remains at the sides above the waist and, under the left arm, the line of the ribbed or beaded edge can be seen as it is carried on into the knot at the waist in front, where the sash is lightly incised.

The beads of the necklace are carved singly, in detail. Four rows are defined of the usual lotus petal, mandrake and date shapes, with intervening cylinder beads. The Aten plaques are evidently threaded into the necklace and resemble glazed examples in the Collection.

There is no suggestion of a plinth. The carving at the back is lighter and less detailed, perhaps because it was intended to stand against or near a wall. The torso suggests it was a portrait of the Queen, but there is no designation.

MOUTH AND CHIN FROM A COLOSSAL STATUE

This lower part of a face from a quartzite statue is approximately twice life size. The break across the chin, which is almost a clean cut as though damaged from one heavy blow, is 9 centimetres wide and 8 centimetres from

14. Lips and chin from one of Akhenaten's colossal statues at Amarna. (H. 14 cm.).

top to bottom. The finished surface of the stone remains on the right side of the broken chin and on the left of the face, along the jaw line to the diagonal break. In his unpublished day-to-day excavation notes from Amarna, Petrie recorded shortly after his arrival that he found in the Palace ruins the lower part of a face of a colossus of Khuanaten [*sic*]. No piece in the Collection other than this corresponds to the description. Pendlebury, from his findings, wrote that the Broad Hall was completely surrounded by colossal statues of the King and Queen, which he estimated were slightly under twice life-size. The Queen's were apparently of sandstone; those of the King of both granite and sandstone.

The fine but not high burnish of the pale red quartzite and the sensitively carved planes of the face give a flesh-like effect. The lips are full and everted; they appear relaxed, despite the fact that—except where they meet on the left side of the face—they are chipped. The curving line where the lips close, and the rise in the cheek by the diagonal break, suggest a faint smile. The chin and jaw line could have terminated in the shape of Akhenaten's prominent chin but would not appear to lead to a pendulous feature.

The life-like carving of the features has an animation, in contrast to the finely carved but immobile majesty of the colossal smiling head of Amenhotep III in the British Museum. This, although stylised in its facial planes, foreshadows the changes which occurred in the Amarna style of carving.[1]

[UC 003]
Provenance: Amarna. Red quartzite. Height left of face 14·0 cm. Width along the left jaw line 14·0 cm. Unpublished. Comparison: [1]British Museum No. 6; *Introductory Guide to the Egyptian Collections*, p. 182, pl. 62, London, 1969.

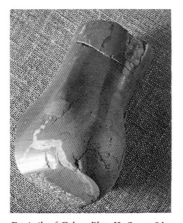

Facsimile of Colour Plate II. See p. 64.

[UC 150]
Provenance: A house in Amarna. Orange-red jasper. Height 12·0 cm. Width 8·0 cm. Across top surface, front to back 6·5 cm. Front transverse surface, top to sole 7·5 cm. Across sole, Width 5·0 cm. Lit. W. M. F. Petrie's unpublished journal from the site, p. 69; J. Samson, *C/A III*, text p. 227, pl. *CVI* (5). Comparison: W. C. Hayes, *Scepter of Egypt, II*, fig. 156, MMA., N.Y., 1968. E. Riefstahl, *AEGG*, Brooklyn Museum, pl. XI, No. 76.

RED JASPER ANKLE AND HEEL

This life-sized red jasper ankle, heel and section of a foot is realistically observed. With a transverse polished surface across the leg where the white gown would reach it, and another sloping across the instep for the front of the foot to be added, it is clearly part of a composite statue; Petrie noted it in his unpublished excavation journal as the largest such piece he remembered.

The ankle bone is strongly but delicately carved and the fibula shaped as though rising from it. At the back the Achilles tendon is shown with detailed planes. The sole of the foot is shaped with a flat base and a ridge round the edge. Above this, up the side of the foot, is a gentle swelling as though from the weight of the body on it. The jasper of the foot has grey streaks in it and is more yellow than the stone at the ankle and above it, which is an orange to red colour. The photograph can only suggest the genius with which the bones, muscles and tendons have been carved. The finish of this glass-like stone has been described as scarcely short of miraculous.

A small, highly polished, curved but uncut piece of darker red jasper in the Collection (UC 111), and a similar piece with part of a mouth carved on it (UC 112) could have come from the same statue. On the latter the lips remain from the centre nearly to the right corner and below them, the highly polished stone is recessed before the beginning of the outward turn towards the chin. Above the lips the surface has broken away, leaving unfinished jasper, as at the back of the fragment.

14b. Back of Tutankhamen's golden
throne (Cairo). (Photo: Griffith Institute)

A LION'S HEAD

This small stone head of a lion is sensitively but boldly carved with a
characteristically leonine mask. The eyes are carved in detail with convex
eyeballs; the nose shaped, and the whiskers incised. Over the head the hair or
mane is stylised into a cap-like covering with a central point on the forehead.

15. *Lion's head shaped to be fixed into a right-angle. (H. 5 cm.).*

[UC 24278] (W)
Provenance: Amarna, S.W. Quarter, N. Suburb (30/240). Painted pumice stone. Length 8·0 cm. Width 6·0 cm. Height 5·0 cm. Unpublished, except for excavation note, J. D. S. Pendlebury, *C/A II*, p. 87 (T.36.57).

The ears are shaped low down on the sides of the head, and the only remains of paint (red) occurs below and behind them.

The muzzle is carved underneath as though to be fitted or slotted onto a horizontal surface, and the back of the head is a smooth vertical plane, which would fit against an upright. The head would have fitted into a corner at the end of the arm of a chair or throne, where it would have made a comfortable hand rest. It is worn smooth on top and, if the paint once covered the head, this too has worn away, perhaps from the contact of a hand. It is reminiscent of the use of lions' heads on thrones and royal chairs from the Old Kingdom onwards. An XVIIIth Dynasty instance on Tutankhamen's golden throne, is in the corner made by the top of the leg and the upright of the arm.

Notes on Monkey Statuettes

MONKEY STATUETTES AND RELIEFS

In a series of 23 unpublished, coloured limestone statuettes of monkeys found by Petrie at Amarna, and two more from the Wellcome Trust, the animals are shown playing the harp, practising acrobatics, eating and drinking, cosseting their young and driving a chariot. Pendlebury believed that some he found were more than a satire on human behaviour and more than just toys, and were in fact caricatures of the royal family at Amarna.[1] A few in the Collection also suggest the enjoyment of them may have been on two levels, as the pranks of monkeys and, as parodies of the current human scenes. The carving of the small pieces, although careless, is in no way amateur, and sculptors of the repetitive scenes in innumerable reliefs may have enjoyed satirising the unusually informal representations of the royal family—the King, for instance, driving his own carriage with the Queen in it, in unprecedented manner.[2] The statuettes have the vitality of Amarna scenes, earlier toys[3] and New Kingdom papyri.[4]

Most of the figures have the remains of paint on them, which, in some, gives a realistic effect. A number combine relief carving with rounded figures; they are heavy and clumsy. Many stand on their own base but some have an upward-curving base and will not stand alone. A number of groups have a hole or holes through them near the base, and, in such examples as the chariot, if a stick were passed through the hole and a wheel added at each end of it, the "toy" could simulate the mobility of the original.

As the statuettes and the reliefs on them are carved both sides, they have been photographed with a mirror reflection.

Comparisons: [1]J. D. S. Pendlebury, *C/A II*, p. 99, pl. XXXI; [2]N. de G. Davies, *RTA*, IV, pl. XX; [3]Monkeys, Old Kingdom, B.M. 11888; MMA, W. C. Hayes, *Scepter of Egypt*, *II*, p. 314, N.Y., 1968; [4]B. M. Papyrus, No. 10016.

TWO MONKEY STATUETTES

The Chariot Driver

On both sides of this painted sunk relief, a monkey is shown driving a horse-drawn chariot, from the same end of the block. The stone on this edge and the top and bottom is smoothed. The block was evidently rectangular as the diagonal break down the middle leaves only the haunch, hind legs and tail of the horse, whose body and head were presumably shown on the missing front fragment.

On the obverse, the bony head and prognathous jaw of the monkey is roughly carved but unmistakably simian. It faces left and its thin body is upright in the chariot. Although the arms are carelessly carved, their action

Plate 16

[UC 029]
Provenance: Amarna. Painted limestone. Height 8·5 cm. Width 8·0 cm. Depth 2·0 cm. Unpublished.

is vigorous, the right uplifted, perhaps with a whip, and the left holding the reins. The horse is galloping. The lines of the wheel and a quiver, an imitation of a real war chariot, are carelessly incised. Traces of pink paint remain on the monkey.

On the reverse, in the mirror, the monkey faces right. Its head and shoulder have been rubbed away, but pink remains on the body and one visible arm, held up as on the other side. The quiver and wheel are incised, but the design is rough and confused. A hole is drilled through the piece near the bottom of the wheel, and if the front of the block had another in that position, two transverse sticks with wheels on them could have made the "chariot" mobile.

16. Monkey statuettes; one monkey drives a chariot, others are at play. The reverse view is shown in the mirror. (H. 8 cm.).

Statuette of Eight Monkeys

Unusually designed with two layers, this statuette shows four small monkeys above four larger ones. Two monkeys are seated side by side each end of the base with their outer arms stretched to meet around a large shape that is dented by their encirclement of it. The shape also bulges above their knees from the pressure of their legs braced against it, and suggests a bag of produce, nuts (?). The four smaller monkeys on the top layer are also two a

[UC 017]
Provenance: Amarna. Painted limestone. Height 9·0 cm. Width 5·6 cm. Depth 2·0 cm. Unpublished.

38

side, three seated and one standing on top of the sack. Their legs also make an impression on it in places, but their arms, although outstretched on one side, are not around it. They could be playing with each other, or about to forage for the produce squeezed up by the elders below. There is a hole through the piece between the smaller monkeys, possibly to clarify the design which is lively and unusual. The limestone has a brown coating with faint traces of red paint on some of the figures.

THREE MONKEY STATUETTES

17. *Three monkey statuettes with young animals, one with a pile of dates(?). The reverse is shown in the mirror. (H. 5·5 to 6·5 cm.).*

Two monkeys in left group

In the pyramidal group on the left, a large monkey, facing right, embraces a baby monkey which faces her while straddling a trussed bird. The piece is rounded and carved on the front and back but not identically. The base is an oval.

The left angle of the design is formed by the sloping back of the larger animal, and part of its head is now broken, as it bends over the smaller animal in its arms. The smaller monkey whose head is missing is crouching with bent arms and legs on the bird, and bending forward, making the sloping angle of the right side. A hole is pierced through the base. With realistic naturalism, the carving expresses a protective, perhaps family affection.

Centre group

In the centre of the plate is a rounded group of a larger monkey facing left, and a smaller one which, on the obverse, clings to an unidentifiable bottle-shaped object. This has a tall oval body in the round, with a rounded

[UC 032]
Provenance: Amarna. Limestone. Height 6·0 cm. Width 6·0 cm. Depth 2·0 cm. Unpublished.

39

top. The oval base is now broken across the front; red paint remains on the figures, particularly on the unidentified shape.

The larger monkey is seated, elbows on knees, with its hands either side of the top of the tall shape, to which its mouth is attached. It might be supposed to be gnawing the stopper off a wine or beer jar, but the smaller monkey clings to the side of this as though it were soft. This, and the overall look of the piece suggests that the larger animal might be kissing the face of an unmodelled figure and that it could be a parody of the many scenes of the King kissing one of his daughters.[1] It bears a striking resemblance to an unfinished statue on this subject. In another monkey statuette in the Collection (UC 020), the snout of the larger animal is unmistakably joined to that of a smaller monkey on its knee.

Monkey with a Pile of Produce

Right of the plate, the monkey, facing left, is seated on an oval base along which its tail lies on the obverse side. Its legs are bent, feet braced against, and right arm round, a pile of dates (?) reaching to its chin. The left forearm is raised, either to steady the pile of fruit or take some to its mouth; in a similar statuette (UC 025) the monkey carries the fruit to its mouth in both hands.

The animal's upright back forms the right edge of the piece, the pile of fruit making the sloping left side. The body is well realised, the eyes carefully carved and the mouth and whiskers incised. The head has been replaced.

Traces of red paint remain on the statuette and the fruit, but this is one of these statuettes which shows signs of having been burnt, possibly after being discarded on one of the waste heaps which were apparently levelled at Amarna, and burnt off from time to time.

[UC 033]
Provenance: Amarna. Painted limestone. Height 6·5 cm. Width 4·0 cm. Depth 2·5 cm. Comparison: [1]M.D.O.G., No. 52, pl. 2. Cairo, Ent. No. 44.866.

[UC 026]
Provenance: Amarna. Painted limestone. Height 5·5 cm. Width 5·0 cm. Depth 1·5 cm. Unpublished.

Reliefs

EARLY STYLE OF AMARNA RELIEF OF NEFERTITI

Although the mannerisms of the early Amarna style coarsen and age Nefertiti's features in this sunk relief, which was evidently carved when she was comparatively young, the rounded forms of her figure convey a flesh-like softness.

18. Early Amarna relief of Nefertiti wearing a Theban wig and disk with horns. (H. 13 cm.).

The Queen faces left on a splinter of marble probably from a temple scene. In the conventional way, her shoulders are shown frontally, and her right breast in profile, but her left breast seems to have been unusually emphasised in a frontal position. A guide-line remains drawn from the left shoulder diagonally across the body. Her left arm is lost and the right one held out, possibly making an offering to the Aten. The uraeus is cursorily incised on a Theban type of wig, surmounted by the disk and horns of Isis. The ear is large and prominent as in the early Amarna reliefs. The bones of the face are modelled and an ageing line drawn from nostril to mouth, another early innovation. The eyebrow is deeply cut but the eye is subtly suggested by "bruising" the stone, perhaps unfinished, but certainly in a shape which is animated by light and shadow. The heavily carved profile has an outer line round the lips and makes strong shadows which give depth and form to the relief.

This is an example which reveals the change that took place in the Amarna age, from the previous artistic conception of carving religious scenes for the darkness of traditional temples, to the new demand for scenes dedicated to the sun in the direct light of unroofed buildings. The background shapes, the handling of the features, the heavily cut and angled outlines of the body, in contrast to the lighter stress laid on the crown and the even fainter lines of the wig, give a deliberate emphasis in a bright light. The carving is probably contemporary with the Queen's portrait on the balustrade from the Palace, but the handling of Amarna carving in religious scenes appears to be related to their individual significance and the effect of light and shadow.

[UC 038]
Provenance: Amarna. Marble. Height 13·0 cm. Width 4·5 cm. Lit. J. Samson, C/A III, p. 224, pl. CV (10).

Plate 20
(particularly visible on Plates 24 and 25)

NEFERTITI IN HER TALL CROWN

In this bold ink drawing of Nefertiti in her prime the Queen wears the tall crown as in the best known Berlin portrait. Her profile, facing right, is on an unevenly squared piece of limestone with bevelled edges which may have been prepared for the master sketch. The edge behind the Queen is broken.

The portrait is outlined with masterly fluency. Lines running down the crown and around its edges and the uraeus are faultlessly placed. The almond shaped outline of the eye has the cosmetic line added and the line of a fold in the eye-lid touched in. One continuous brush stroke sweeps across the cap band on the brow and down the profile. Guide lines mark the lower plane of the jaw, two neck wrinkles, and the back of the neck which gives the recognisable forward poise of the Queen's head, all apparently for a sculptor to follow.

Carving has been started on the nostril, lips and chin, but false lines by the ear, perhaps carved by a pupil, are not properly placed for it or for an ear-ring and may have caused the work to be abandoned.

The drawing has the naturalism of the portrait heads in the round from Thutmose's studio, and it reveals the artistic certainty underlying such masterpieces.

[UC 011]
Provenance: Amarna. Limestone, with ink drawing, and carving. Height 8·5 cm. Width 7·0 cm. Lit. P. T/A., p. 30, par. 72. J. Samson, C/A III, p. 225, pl. CV (3).

19. *Nefertiti in her tall crown typical of many of her portraits from Amarna.* (H. 8·5 cm.).

ROYAL FIGURE ON A PALACE BALUSTRADE

This heavy alabaster section is from one of the balustrades that bordered the ramps in the central palace. It is a sunk relief, *en creux*, with the familiar scene of Akhenaten and Nefertiti offering to the Aten, followed by Meritaten, playing her sistrum. All face right and stand under the beneficent rays of the Aten. The relief, although broken above the King's shoulders, clearly shows the deeply cut ribs on the streamer which hangs down from his head-dress. On the King's upper arms, chest and waist, double cartouches are incised, showing the early form of the Aten names. The Queen wears an informal "bag" wig. Between her two uplifted hands, she offers an unguent vase which is blessed by a hand of the Aten; another touches her head, while, between them, a third brings the *ʿankh* to the uraeus on her brow. Seven other rays ending in hands descend to the three unguent vases on the offering table in front of the King. The two nearest the centre hang almost straight as though from the sun's disk (above the break). The depth of the cutting, and the angling of the carving is varied to achieve the full effect of light and shadow on the scene.

Before the Queen's skirt is inscribed:—

Nfr-nfrw-itn Nfrt-iti ʿnḫ ḏt nḥḥ.

"Nefer-neferu-aten Nefertiti, living forever and ever."

Above her head are the ends of two columns of large hieroglyphs, ending:

1. ....*n t3wy*   2. ....*ḏt nḥḥ*

" ....(Mistress?) of the Two Lands"   .... "for ever and ever".

Over the princesses, a vertical column reads:

..... *Mrt-(itn) ms.n ḥmt-nswt wrt Nfr-nfrw-itn Nfrt-iti ʿnḫ.ti ḏt nḥḥ*

". . . . Merit(aten), born of the Great Royal Wife, Nefer-neferu-aten, Nefertiti, living forever and ever."

This section of the balustrade, originally in fragments, has been somewhat clumsily restored with plaster.

[UC 401]
Provenance: Central Palace at Amarna; early years Egyptian alabaster. Height 56·0 cm. Width 52·0 cm. Lit. W. M. F. Petrie, *T/A*, p. 8, pl. XII (3); p. 11 (19), pl. XII (4). J. D. S. Pendlebury, *C/A III* p. 66 and p. 77, pl. LXIX (4 and 5). Comparisons: [1]Cairo, E. Drioton, *Encyclopédie Photographique de l'Art*, p. 40.

The block was found standing with another in the eastern doorway between the Broad Hall and the first State Apartment. The style of the art, with the disproportionately large hips, narrow waist and thin legs of the King and Queen and the distortion of her features, is little different from the Boundary Stelae. This, with the very childlike figure of Meritaten and the probable position of the balustrade in the palace, suggest it was carved early in the preparation of the city. Other sections of balustrades in limestone, purple sandstone, and black and red granite decorated the ramps leading up to the unusual architectural feature of raised doorways, and this suggests they were emphasised as focal points. They would have enabled Akhenaten and Nefertiti to pause in their long procession through the palace and "appear" above the heads of assembled audiences, as they entered and left the succession of State Apartments leading to the throne, a more intimate version of their royal appearances to the public outside the palace.

This block is roughly squared at the bottom, and at both sides, to fit beside other sections of the balustrade. On this one, the family stands on a gently rising line; in a similar Cairo block, the base-line is a descending one, parallel to the top.[1] As on the Deir-el-Bahri ramps, the supporting walls evidently took the change in gradient, leaving the balustrades at a fixed height. Comparisons show they reached a height of 1·18 metres.

20. The King, Queen and princess probably Meritaten, shown on an alabaster balustrade from the Central Palace, offering to the Aten. (H. 56 cm.).

44

FIGURE OF NEFERTITI FROM MEMPHIS

This early portrait of Nefertiti in coloured sunk relief was found by Petrie on the site of the Temple of Ptah in Memphis. Its style and dress distinguish it from early portraits of the Queen in the same pose from Thebes and Amarna, and it appears to be a rare example of an Amarna royal portrait from the north.

The limestone block is squared on the right side, at the base and on the top which is chipped, but the left side has been completely broken away. The Queen, facing left, stands at the end of what was almost certainly an Aten scene, with a slim column behind her. The damage on the left has removed the front of her face, broken the right shoulder, and taken the right arm, lower left arm and the left of her semi-profile body, which the end of the block cuts at hip level. She wears the long Theban type of wig with a fillet which was probably surmounted by a diadem. The hair is carved in detail; one lappet falls over her left breast and the rest behind her left shoulder. The ear is large and, typical of the early period, is shown prominently on top of the wig. There are traces of the uraeus on the brow and shapes which, by comparison with other reliefs (especially one in the Cleveland Museum), suggest that there was an Aten hand in front of it and possibly another carrying the ʿankh to her nose.[1]

21. This figure of Nefertiti is rare because Petrie found it at Memphis and she wears a skirt which differs from her portraits from Thebes and Amarna. (H. 20 cm.).

The top of the brow, the almond eye, and simply carved eyebrow, although chipped, are clearly visible. The front of the face is missing, but if it was originally carried forward on the same plane as the remaining cheek, it would seem to have been shown as smooth and more fitting to a young woman than to the gaunt and lined portraits of the young Queen from the southern capitals. The frontal shoulders and three-quarters right breast are rounded; the upper left arm, bent across the body to the waist, was probably raised with an offering to the Aten in the Queen's hands, as in so many examples.[2] On the arm is a pair of cartouche-plaques with the early form of the Aten name used before year 9; a similar pair on the right breast are partly broken away by the damage to the shoulder.

The dress is not typical of a Theban or of an Amarna Queen's robe. There is no suggestion of a necklace, and the pleated sash around her waist with a cross-ribbed tie falling from the centre is reminiscent of the style of sash worn by Menkheper, Mayor of Memphis, in the previous reign.[3] It presumably held up her skirt.

The smashing of the left side of the block may have obliterated the figure of the King who usually precedes her, and certainly all signs of the Aten. The gash behind her head occurs in the position where an Aten hand often appears, and was probably to obliterate the symbol.

Pale red paint remains on her face and body and the portrait gives an impression of relaxed elegance rather than the more rigid crudity of early reliefs of the Queen from Thebes and Amarna.

[UC 037]
Provenance: Temple of Ptah, Memphis. Amarna Period. Painted limestone. Height 20·0 cm. Width 18·5 cm. Lit. W. M. F. Petrie, *Riqqeh and Memphis, VI*, p. 32, pl. LIV (9), 1915. Comparisons: [1]*Cleveland Museum Bulletin*, No. 59, 186, fig. 6, Jan. 1968; [2]J. D. S. Pendlebury, *C/A III*, pl. LXVI (1); [3]W. C. Hayes, *Scepter of Egypt, II*, p. 272, fig. 166, MMA., N.Y., 1968.

SITAMEN FROM THEBES

[UC 14373]
Provenance: Temple of Amenophis II/ III, Thebes, Dynasty XVIII, c. 1380 B.C. Painted sandstone. Height 51·0 cm. Width 49·0 cm. Lit. W. M. F. Petrie, *Six Temples at Thebes*, pp. 6 and 11, pl. VI (8), 1897.

22. Sitamen from Thebes. (H. 51 cm.)

46

On this large sandstone block, the *bas-relief* carving of a Queen is unfinished. Above her head, in the lower left corner of a broken cartouche, are the back and legs of the *s3* bird and part of a *t* from the name Sitamen. Beside it is the bottom of a column of inscription with only the *t* remaining legible. Above this and at an angle down the right side, the block is broken. The left side and lower edge are squared.

Sitamen faces right. She wears the vulture head-dress with the head and body of the bird carved in detail, but the lappet, which falls from the head-dress down on to her breast, and the three-cornered "streamer", which flares out from it at the back, are only blocked in, with traces of blue paint still remaining on them. The Queen wears a necklace of which only the edges are carved, the rows being shown by blue painted loops. Over her shoulders are the straps of her Theban gown from which her left breast protrudes by her left arm near the break in the stone, beyond which was presumably her sheath-like dress. Her face is carved without planes; the profile is clearly cut, the nostril modelled, and there is a trace of a smile on the full lips. The chin is firm and the carriage of the head regal. The eye is merely a recessed oval, with the cosmetic line from the outer edge, and the eyebrow raised in *bas-relief*. The Queen carries the royal "flail" with the lily terminal, which falls along the top line of her left arm.

Except for this queenly pose, the details of the portrait closely resemble the more finished, painted limestone relief of Hatshepsut's mother, 'Aḥmose, at Deir-el-Bahri, but both her arms drop straight down from her shoulders. The shallow *bas-relief* carving of Sitamen's portrait is in the tradition of XVIIIth Dynasty temple reliefs, and the vulture head-dress of a royal heiress, God's Wife of Amen, is the same as that worn by pre-Amarna Queens of this Dynasty. The relief was found by Petrie in the Theban temple of Amenophis II, which was later remodelled by Amenophis III; this relief has been associated with his daughter, Sitamen. Described as both his daughter and his wife, her rôle in her father's entourage was evidently that of royal heiress. Possibly an official marriage was arranged between them, perhaps to secure a male heir, as Àkhenaten and Nefertiti apparently had only daughters, and Queen Ty, although so powerful, was born a commoner.

The carving may have been taken over by Amenophis III, by adding a relevant inscription. So reminiscent of queens who occur earlier in the Dynasty, it provides a contrast to royal portraiture later in his reign and in the Amarna period. Sitamen, the royal heiress, is monumentally majestic, impersonal, and ageless.

PROFILE OF AKHENATEN

On a limestone slab, squared both sides and at the bottom but broken diagonally across the top, is the lower half of the profile of a King in shallow sunk relief. The break on the left is above the ear and, on the right, above the nostril. The King faces right, and strongly resembles portraits of Akhenaten.

The carving is in the best tradition of Amarna reliefs. The nostril is sensitive, the lips full but not coarse, and the chin is bony without the exaggeration of the early period. The face is delicately modelled but the

Plate 23

[UC 402]

Provenance: By the sculptor's place near the southern end of the town, Amarna. Limestone. Height 17·0 cm. Width 19·0 cm. Lit. P. *T/A*, p. 31, pl. 1 (5) and p. 11. Comparison: G. Roeder, *Amarna Reliefs aus Hermopolis*, pl. 5, 255-VI, Hildesheim, 1969.

subtle gradation of the planes is masked by the pitted surface of the stone. Two folds are shown on the front of the neck in Amarna tradition, but the front line of the neck is not continued down to the break in the stone. On the left, the ear is less well carved than the rest of the face, with an unduly deep rounded cavity, similar to those which were shown pierced through the lobe, needed for the shanks of Amarna ear-rings. On this ear, however, the lobe is not fully carved. Behind the ear is the base of the Blue Crown and the turn at the back of the thin neck.

23. Profile of Akhenaten in the Amarna style without the exaggeration of the early Karnak portraits. (H. 17 cm.).

Petrie records the finding of the piece by the sculptor's place near the south end of the town (Thutmose's(?)), and describes it as "the head of Akhenaten on a slab which does not appear to have come from any building and is probably a trial (piece)." The unfinished line at the base of the neck gives it this appearance and, found so near the studio, it may have been a "copy book" sample. It is comparable with a relief of Akhenaten from Hermopolis. Although this is on a larger block with more of the King's body showing, and it has more stylised carving, there are sufficient parallels for both pieces to have been based on the same or similar model of the King's profile.

48

A QUEEN OFFERS LIBATION TO THE ATEN

On an unevenly broken block of purple quartzite, a Queen, probably Nefertiti, is following a King whose shoulder and the streamers from his crown are in front of her. The stone is finely prepared and polished and the carving is notable for a combination of techniques giving emphasis from strong light and shadow.

The Queen faces left and in her upraised hands offers to the Aten a typical libation vessel with a short spout. Two rays from the Sun-God descend

49

[UC 040]
Provenance: Amarna, Great Temple (?). Purple quartzite. Height 15·2 cm. Width 10·0 cm. Lit. J. Samson, C/A III, p. 225, pl. CV (6). Comparison: J. D. S. Pendlebury, C/A III, p. 11, Great Temple.

diagonally across the surface, the upper one with a hand on the end blessing the uraeus on the Queen's brow; the lower ray passes behind the Queen's head, giving a three-dimensional effect. The broken right edge of the block cuts across the wig and face of the Queen in front of the ear. The head is carved in sunk relief.

The front of the "Nubian" wig and the uraeus catch the light. The top outline of the profile, eyebrow and eye are deeply carved to give deep shadow in a top, left light, but this illumines the brow and eyelid and the lines under the nostril and chin and between the lips. The planes of the face are natural without the sunken and lined appearance of the exaggerated "Amarna" style, and allows only a slight shadow under the cheek-bone. The Aten rays are deeply cut, and the straight sides catch light on one edge. Further emphasis is given to the religious meaning of the relief by combining different carving techniques around the offering. The Queen's uplifted forearms are rounded between the sunken edges, but her left hand, which supports the libation vessel, is in raised relief against the recessed stone of the streamers from the King's crown. The right hand is in sunk relief, but raised along the fore-finger, and these variations would focus the eye on the offering in any light. Two Aten plaques on the Queen's right arm are uninscribed.

Pendlebury believed this may be a fragment from the great "purple" stela of which he found many pieces in the unroofed temple, where the combined carving techniques would show to advantage, and give emphasis to the religious ritual.

A LIBATION OFFERING TO THE ATEN

In a painted relief on this roughly rectangular limestone fragment, which is broken on all four edges, significance is given to a libation which is being offered to the Aten, by employing various carving techniques, similar to the offering above.*

*Plate 24

[UC 24281] (W)
Provenance: The Broad Hall, central palace, Amarna. Painted limestone. Height 15·0 cm. Width 14·0 cm. J. D. S. Pendlebury's excavation reference, C/A III, (265), p. 68.

25. Both the carving of this relief and the painting of the sun's rays red against the white limestone intensify this libation offering to the Aten. (H. 15 cm.).

The neck of the libation vase is broken at the top left of the block, but the body of the vase is held upright on an elongated hand with long fingers and back-turned top joints, typical of royal hands in so many reliefs at Amarna. Three rays from the Aten descend diagonally towards the left, with narrowing distances between them as they near the centre (under the sun's disk). The ray on the left passes behind the vessel and the hand, and gives a three-dimensional effect that is heightened by the rounded shape of the vase which is recessed at the sides. Between recessed outlines, the sun's rays are rounded, and traces remain on them of the red paint; this stresses the pattern they make against the very white smooth limestone. Colour is used here to give the emphasis achieved by the deep squared cutting of the rays on the offering above. The hand and fingers are in sunk relief, with red paint remaining around them, but by recessing the bottom of the vessel, the thumb is shown in *bas-relief*, so as to catch the light from all angles.

Plate 24

The relief was found in the unroofed Broad Hall of the central palace, and increases the evidence of the skill which went into the royal and religious scenes at Amarna.

AN EARLY AMARNA PORTRAIT OF A PRINCESS

[UC 083]
Provenance: Amarna. Diorite. Height 15·0 cm. Width 10·0 cm. Unpublished.

26. Although she is only small and young the angularity of this early Amarna portrait of a princess, ages her. (H. 15 cm.) Unpublished.

51

This angular carving of a princess, on a heavy, unevenly broken block of diorite with only part of the right edge unbroken, has all the signs of one of the earliest carvings in the building of Amarna. It probably shows Meritaten, the eldest princess; she is at the end of a scene, closely following her mother, whose gown, apparently below the hips, can be seen in front of the princess next to and above her head. The carving of what was presumably Nefertiti's figure appears to be on a big scale; the princess's figure is relatively small, suggesting that she was a young child. Her exaggerated and projecting adult features and her attenuated body with its almost wizened appearance, so like the disproportion of the portraits from the early Aten days at Thebes, endorses the early date.

Although so young, she is elaborately dressed, perhaps attending an official Aten ceremony. She holds the princess' sistrum in her right hand just above her head; the left arm is hanging in a typical manner by her side. Both arms are match-stick thin and her waist is little broader. She wears the side-lock of youth, a collar-necklace and a gown draped across her chest with pleats down the skirt. The block is broken at her knees. Above her head an ḥ sign remains, from the prayer for eternal life at the end of a column of inscription. The angularity of this figure can be compared with the more

Plate 27

flowing lines of the princess in the scene on a column from the central palace, for which there is evidence of a later date.

A PRINCESS FROM A CENTRAL PALACE COLUMN

In Akhenaten's central palace, described by Pendlebury as the largest secular building in the ancient world and the only one built of stone, he found this fragment in the first inner court, south of the Broad Hall.[1] The highly polished, light honey coloured quartzite is part of a band that encircled a column some two feet in diameter.

The princess is carved in low relief and faces left. She was evidently part of a scene of the royal family as described by Petrie on the bands encircling the columns in the harem court.[2] Her right arm is raised, presumably to hold a sistrum above her head; her left hangs down by her side. She wears the side-lock of youth over an apparently shaven head or possibly on a cap (with the side-lock attached to it). A large collar-necklace hangs over her gown which is draped across her left breast with the pleats gathered at the waist and hanging down over the hips, leaving the front of the figure bare. The sloping break in the stone is under the buttock and above the knees.

Despite the heavy face, and the disproportion of the attenuated stock pose of the figure, the style of the carving suggests it was a later work than that of the princess on page 51; the less angular lines of the figure offer a greater contrast than can be explained by the softer stone alone, and there are pointers to it being carved at a later period at Amarna, when the royal daughters were growing up. The princess on the fragment is possibly Meritaten, as she appears to be immediately following her mother, whose robe can be seen on the left lower corner of the fragment, and she is taller in relation to this indication of her mother's figure than she was on page 51. Behind her is apparently the elbow of another princess with arm upheld, presumably with a sistrum, who is also relatively tall. Furthermore, the fragment was found

[UC 24279] (W)
Provenance: First State Apartment of the Central Palace, Amarna. Yellow quartzite. Height 17·0 cm. Width 14·0 cm. Lit. ¹J. D. S. Pendlebury's excavation note, C/A III, (No. 100), p. 68. Comparison: ²P. T/A, p. 10, pl. 1. Unpublished.

Plate 26

Plate 26

in the Court where Pendlebury uncovered the foundations of a temporary brick structure which he identified as the office of the architect who was directing the building of the State Apartments. He believed that these could not have been finished before year 9 and as this Court would have had to wait completion until after the brick shelter was removed, it was possibly one of the last sections to be finished. If the fragment belonged to the court in which it was found, it would endorse the assessment of a middle date for the piece on grounds of style and the relative sizes of the princesses.

27. From a scene on a Central Palace column. This princess is holding up a sistrum. The flowing lines of the figure suggest it is later than plate 26. (H. 17 cm.).

TWO OFFERING BEARERS

Two offering bearers in this painted, sunk relief face right, as they carry fruit and flowers to an altar or at a temple ceremony. The block is dressed stone at the top and on the right but unevenly broken at the bottom and left side. The scene shows a number of the innovations that characterise Amarna art.

28. Two offering bearers with fruit and flowers. (H. 33 cm.).

The bearers are carved with the shaven heads of temple attendants and wear the usual pleated skirt and central tie, but, typical of the best Amarna scenes, although they were presumably subordinate figures in a scene among many officials, they are carved as individuals. Both men are shown with their slightly differing heads and faces in profile and their skulls recessed around the ear, which emphasises their bare heads. Their frontal shoulders and nearly profile bodies retain the conventions of traditional Egyptian art. But although this subject in previous reigns is mostly shown by repetitive figures carrying different offerings, here, the man on the left bends forward more than the

54

other bearer and although they carry virtually the same produce, the design is varied and carved to suggest movement and depth.

The bearer on the left holds in his right hand a large XVIIIth Dynasty bouquet sheath made with layers of stalks bound together. This rests on his right shoulder and fits behind his head, accentuating the projecting back of his skull, giving a three-dimensional effect. From the top of the sheath a large papyrus flower emerges, notched around the rim and recessed at both sides giving another illusion of depth. This, though partly broken away, is flanked right and left by two buds. The man's left arm is held out before him with a basket or tray of offerings balanced on his nearly horizontal forearm. On this tray are two layers of figs on top of three pomegranates, all upright in profile. This pile of fruit almost covers the body of the second bearer who is shorter, which gives a degree of perspective to the design. From the top of his right shoulder and presumably held in his right hand are three rectangular stylised bouquet "cones" with slightly curved tops designed as though fitting into one another; these are also recessed both sides. The use of such floral cones is apparently demonstrated on the raised border of the stela, where lotuses and buds emerge from the shapes, and loops. From the cones rises a larger papyrus head than on the left, notched at the rim, recessed at both sides and flanked by two buds.

The tray carried by this bearer and some of the produce on it was apparently continued over the edge of the block into the next one, suggesting well fitted masonry minimising the crack between. On the tray are horizontal layers of bread (?), under three layers of upright figs, topped by a large bouquet of papyrus flowers with the stalks twisted and bound into a loop and then hanging down each side of the fruit. From the trays hang branches of leaves. There are traces of red paint on these and occasional touches remaining on the figures.

Across the top of the limestone is a line possibly dividing this from a register above. If these bearers are part of an Aten ritual with the royal family shown in the relatively large proportion in which they appear in the Amarna tombs, the scale of the relief suggests a very large and extensive scene.[1] If they formed part of the preparation of an altar for royal worship, the scale indicates its importance, perhaps in a temple.

The movement in this composition in which the bearers appear to be pressing forward highlights the difference between them and offering bearers in Theban tombs like Ramose's in the previous reign where they are shown in a repetitive line of stereotyped faces and figures like a design in a beautiful frieze.[2] In this scene the forward impetus is suggested by the pose of the figures and intensified by the angles of the shapes between them which mostly point forward. This action in the composition, the individualism of the figures, and the illusion of depth inherent in the placing of objects, the recession of their sides and the diminishing size of the man further from the front, show some of the innovations in the art of the Amarna period.

[UC 405]
Provenance: Amarna. Painted limestone. Height 33·0 cm. Width 33·0 cm. Depth 7·5 cm. Unpublished. Comparisons: [1]N. de G. Davies, *RTA, II*, pl. XVIII, London, 1905; [2]N. de G. Davies, *Tomb of Vizier Ramose*, pl. XLIV and XLVI, London, 1941.

Plate 55a

FIGURE FROM THE TOMB OF AY

The unfinished figure of a servant facing left on this roughly squared block of limestone has the remains of yellow paint on it which evidently once covered the figure. The face in profile is simply carved; the nose is shaped but the eye and mouth little more than incised, although the expression is one of animation undestroyed by the flaked and chipped stone. The head is lifted slightly, the right arm, carved to the elbow, is raised in evident acclaim and the left, carved to the wrist, swings out behind the figure. A "Nubian" wig is shaped with a long back-line; the figure wears the pubic sheath with a narrow tie round the waist as worn by soldiers, sentries, charioteers and grooms. The shoulders are shown frontally and the abdomen and legs in three-quarter view, but the pose is active, looking or perhaps even moving to the left.

29. An unfinished but welcoming figure from the tomb of Ay. (H. 29 cm.).

Petrie described the block as one of a curious class he found in the city, carved on slabs of limestone rudely smoothed at the sides but rounded at the corners which would preclude a good join.[1] He did not know that the tomb robbers had squared the reliefs they hacked from the tomb walls and apparently dropped some of the blocks in the plain. This figure has been traced to a scene on the north wall of Ay's tomb. It was removed between 1843-45, when it was included *in situ* in the drawings for the *Denkmäler* of Lepsius, and 1891-2, when Petrie found it in the city.

The figure is one of a group welcoming Ay as he returns from court laden with honours bestowed by the King and Queen in the previous scene. The three figures nearest Ay were damaged, but this one, perhaps a groom in the service of Ay, the King's Master of Horse, was completely hacked out. The workmanship is rough, the figure unimportant, but it has the involvement typical in crowd scenes at Amarna, and expresses the movement of a genuine participant in a moment of rejoicing.

[UC 409]
Provenance: Amarna. Painted limestone. Height 29·0 cm. Width 24·0 cm. Lit. [1]P. *T/A.*, 11, pl. XI.

A FOOD CARRIER

Although the shaven hair of this man carrying provisions on his head suggests he may be bringing them to an Aten altar in a temple, it is also possible he was carrying food in a palace scene. The figure faces left in a coloured sunk relief on a jagged block of limestone probably hacked from a wall; the surface is badly damaged. The block is broken in front of and behind the figure, above the provisions, and below the face.

30. In this relief the pile of food on the bearer's head is carved into the register above him, an Amarna variation. (H. 9·5 cm., W. 15 cm.).

The modelled features are Egyptian. The slightly turned up nose and thick nostril in the profile which is carved with an open mouth, has a coarseness accentuated by a lump of stone left between the lips. The oval eye is recessed, enabling a deep shadow from the brow, and a highlight on the lid. The skull is recessed around the ear which is roughly carved. At the back of the head is the beginning of the neck; in front, the profile ends at the chin. The provisions of two loaves under a fish (?) are set, perhaps carelessly or for purposes of design, on the back half of the man's head. They appear to extend into the register above the figure, suggested by two horizontal lines across the block in front of the bottom loaves, behind which the surface of the stone is missing. This varying of a composition by extending the forms across the rigid register-lines is one of the innovations at Amarna which gives the reliefs their liveliness. In the top left corner above the lines is unidentifiable carving, with red and yellow paint. Red and yellow paint remain on the provisions and red on the head.

The block has not been squared like those plundered from the tombs and its condition suggests it may have been shattered when quarried from a wall in the city. Little of the surface stone remains around the carving except behind the head, where it is angled in a forward point. The relief is more crudely presented than the offering bearers, but the incisive design expresses action.

FOREIGNERS ON A LIMESTONE BALUSTRADE

Decorated on both sides with a frieze of foreigners, probably captives, this carved block of limestone with the smoothed top is apparently the end block of a balustrade, possibly from one of the many ramps or stairways of the central palace. It has one end bevelled and the other roughly flattened. The rounded or "roll" top with the ridge at the sides is typical of the larger balustrades with decorated sides, found in varying stone, as discussed on page 44. On this less important limestone example, the stone at the top of the finished end slopes outwards to meet a smoothed vertical, while the other end is roughly squared, presumably to fit against the next segment. The work is roughly executed.

The parallel sides are decorated with the painted heads of foreigners in coarse, sunk relief. They face away from the bevelled end, presumably in a procession along the balustrade, and as the height of the block is only some 7 centimetres, it can be assumed that the rest of their figures was carved on the upright sides now broken away.

On the obverse, is the top of the head of a Libyan, broken from below his ear. In front of the ear is the side-lock, and rising from the top of his head, are the two feathers of his head-dress with the streamer falling down the back. Only the brow of his face remains. There are traces of red paint on the head. Behind him is the front half of a negro's head, with part of the hair, the brow, nose and upper lip, but the cheek has broken away. The centre of the head reaches the finished edge of the section. Red paint remains in squares incised on his head, suggesting crinkly hair or a wig. On the reverse is the whole of a profile head of a negro, with the same squared head-dress and remains of red paint on it. The lips are thick, nose spreading and brow receding and he wears the large round ear-ring hanging from his ear. The block is broken at the base of his neck. Behind him is an indistinguishable curved shape, possibly of a partial figure like the one ending the procession on the obverse.

[UC 017]
Provenance: Amarna. Painted limestone. Height 9·5 cm. Width 15·0 cm. Lit. J. Samson, *C/A III*, p. 227, pl. CVI (3).

[UC 069]
Provenance: Amarna. Painted limestone relief. Bevelled end to unfinished surface 11·0 cm. Front surface width 12·5 cm. Height 7·0 cm. Diameter across roll top to side ridges 12·0 cm.

Plate 31

Plate 32

The working of the stone of this block is unusually poor, possibly showing haste in finishing parts of the buildings which were not the State Apartments or important sections, but the national characteristics of the foreigners are appreciated and faithfully represented.

PROFILE OF A MAN

Petrie found this profile relief, which is on a fine piece of limestone, at a sculptor's workshop near the south end of the town, possibly Thutmose's. The head faces left and retains an arresting distinction despite a joined break, across the stone at eye level, and other fractures.

The wig is a typical Amarna shape with the point in this case by the front of the neck. The features are not without resemblance to the royal family but no insignia is shown and it is unlikely to be Queen Ty to whom it was once assigned. The nose is carved with care, the lips droop slightly and a downward line is drawn from the outer corner; the chin and jaw line are well defined. The eye is carved with the particular detail found in good Amarna reliefs. The eyebrow is recessed and the eyelid shown by an outward turn over the almond-shaped eye. The planes of the face mark the cheek bone.

On the reverse are trials of features, a profile and hieroglyphs. Two separate eyes are carved, one in the form used in the profile and the other perhaps by a pupil. There is the ovoid head and profile of an Amarna princess; three pairs of full lips have been carved, one possibly by the master and two with less success. Of two *nb* signs, one shows the weave of the basket.

60

TWO PROFILES ON A TRIAL PIECE

Two profile reliefs of young men facing right have been carved on a block of limestone squared at the right and top and bottom, but broken on the left side. The lower profile is more expertly carved. The outline is faultless; the wig is firmly placed by a line at the top across the brow and another down the face and neck; a line under the recessed eyebrow divides it from the eyelid over the almond-shaped eye. The nose and full lips are modelled and the planes of the face skilfully shown in a young and fairly full cheek.

On the profile above, the same shaped wig is fully but unevenly outlined. Although the features are carved on the same model as below, which might be the master's copy, they lack the fineness. The surface of the stone of this head is more spotted than below, which to some extent masks the planes of the face, but these apparently have not been fully understood by the artist; for instance, the curved line above the lip lacks meaning.

[UC 037]
Provenance: Amarna. Limestone. Height 23·0 cm. Width 18·5 cm. Lit. J. Samson, *C/A III*, p. 225, pl. CV (1).

34. Two profiles on a trial piece. (H. 23 cm.).

SCULPTOR'S STUDIES OF HANDS

The limestone block used as a trial piece for these studies of hands was badly broken at the top and left sides which have been mended with plaster. The right side and bottom of the block are squared. The studies are of three left hands, holding the roll or 'kerchief, which projects from under the little finger that is clenched, with the rest of the fingers in the palm of the hand.

The plaster covers a hand on the bottom left of the block except for the fleshy lower part of the palm, the wrist bone and lower arm which are life-like and make the example on its right look wooden. In this, the four fingers clasp the roll which is shown unfinished beyond the little finger; the thumb bends over the first finger but the palm reflects none of the pressure from the finger and the whole is carved without much indication of muscle or bone. The nails are shown in great detail with a double line encircling the quick.

[UC 2234]
Provenance: Amarna. Limestone. Height 17·0 cm. Width 14·0 cm. Lit. M. Murray, *Egyptian Sculpture*, pl. IV, London, 1930. Comparison: Peterson, *Jaarbericht van het Voorazi-atisch Egyptisch Genootschap ex Orient Lux*, pl. X (E).

35. Sculptor's studies of hands. (H. 17 cm.).

Above this, the clenched hand in the same position has been given more shape in its palm and apparently had a wrist bone, but the stone here is broken. The top of the thumb is lost. The fingers are shown as pressing into the centre of the hand and the roll appears to be held by them but is in-expertly dealt with and where it emerges from under four fingers of nearly the same length gives the impression of a fifth finger. The nails are carved but not all with the detail of the hand below it.

Despite the apparently cursory treatment of some hands, even on major figures in Amarna reliefs, they were clearly studied in detail.

62

THE VARIED CARVING OF HIEROGLYPHS

The hieroglyphs carved on these two fragments of inscriptions on finely grained and highly polished quartzite, probably formed a part of the royal titulary. On the left the quail-chick, *w*, with part of the *šwt* plant, was possibly from *nsw* "King of Upper Egypt", while on the right is the pintail duck, perhaps part of *s3-rᶜ* "the son of the sun" from Akhenaten's name.

The carving of the chick, which faces right, and the stem of the plant, is deep and straight sided, casting heavy shadows which would embolden a description to be seen from afar on an outside wall. The shoots each side of the stem are slender and graceful but catch the light on one edge. This bold treatment needs little detail within the outlines, and the base of the stem and the chick are only slightly modelled; the bird's beak is a thin incised line. Standing on a base-line the chick is given the perkiness of a small bird.

[UC 084 and 74]
Provenance: Amarna. Left fragment, pink quartzite. Height 11·5 cm. Width 9·5 cm. Right fragment, red quartzite. Height 12·0 cm. Width 7·5 cm. Unpublished.

In contrast, the pintail duck is flat footed and has the suggestion of a strut along its base-line. It faces right. The style of carving between two horizontal lines, with the remains of hieroglyphs in the lower register suggests that the inscription is part of one from the pedestal of a statue, or perhaps an indoor wall to be seen at close quarters. For this the outlines are shallower and the edges slightly turned back so that the light falls on the fuller and more detailed modelling of the bird's head, wing and breast, as well as the tail feathers which are partly lost by damage to the stone.

36. Examples of methods of carving hieroglyphs from two different sites. (H. 11·5 cm., W. 9·5 cm.; H. 12 cm., W. 7·5 cm.).

I. Head of Nefertiti with preparation for tall crown to be added in another material. (H. 6·5 cm.).

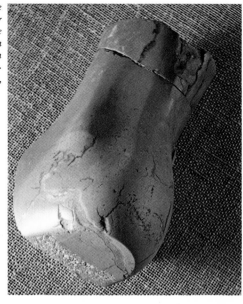

II. Back of an ankle and heel in red jasper from a composite statue with robes in another stone as on the back of Tutankhamen's throne, plate 14b. (H. 12 cm.).

IV. Small wooden figure overlaid with gold, possibly from a piece of furniture. Found at Qurneh, near Thebes. (H. 7·3 cm.).

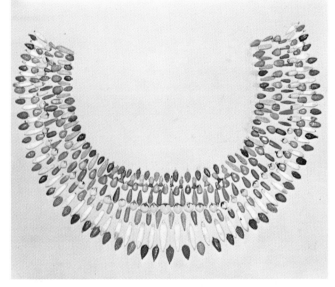

III. Composed of faience beads found separately at Amarna this necklace is assembled on the lines of those worn by both men and women. The beads include grapes, green leaves, green and blue cornflowers, red poppy petals, blue "drops," yellow mandrake fruits, red oval "dates" and white lotus petals, some tipped with blue. (L. longest white petal 4·5 cm. Shortest cornflower 1·5 cm.).

V. Figures of princesses—red moulded glass. (H. 9 cm.).

INK SKETCH OF A STALKING BABOON

This apparently casual record in ink of a baboon prowling on all-fours has deft certainty and the economy of excellence that places it with the world's great sketches. Taking advantage of the smooth surface of a block of fine limestone, the artist has made a free sketch of the animal moving stealthily along to the right. One unbroken brush stroke runs from the tip of its tail along the back and down the right leg. The characteristics of its head and body are unmistakable and achieved with seven or eight strokes.

Many formal designs on walls, where drawings were prepared for the sculptor to carve, lack the immediacy of this quick sketch, but this lacks nothing of the observation and inspired line of the best work of the ancient Egyptian draughtsmen.

37. Ink sketch of a stalking baboon. (L. of drawing 4·2 cm.).

[UC 1585]
Provenance: Amarna. Ink sketch on limestone. The block, Height 7·5 cm. Width 16·0 cm. The length of baboon, Length 4·2 cm. Tail 5·0 cm. Lit. J. Samson, *C/A III*, p. 228.

65

Inlays

TWO ROYAL INLAYS WITH ROUND EDGED CARVING

Both these portraits are carved in the manner customary for stone inlays except that, on one the stone is worked around the front edge of the profile, with the same perfection as on the surface which suggests the turn of the face was meant to be seen. They would not have been easy to inlay flat into **Plate 38** a wall like the head on p. 68, but could have been set with the front edge left above the surface.

38. Part of a royal inlay with carving round the edge. (H. 6 cm.).

In the broken fragment which faces right, the carving and colour continues for half a centimetre round the edge with the same finish as on the rest of the surface. The lips are coloured a soft red and rounded as though they were to lie against the surface rather than sink into it; the chin bulges at the back before it is flattened, which would keep the inlay raised. The shadow cast by the raised profile would have given it the depth which the relief carvers at

Amarna were seeking in their varied cutting. The surface of the stone has a warmer tone than the yellower colour at the back, probably from the effect of its extremely fine finish or perhaps from the faint remains of flesh colouring. No photograph fully shows the subtle modelling of the flesh over the chin or the soft planes of the jawline. The relaxed, sensuous, edged lips are slightly drooping at the corners with the fold of a half smile typical of some of the Amarna royal portraits. The contours of this face are softer and more feminine than those in the other head, and suggest it was part of an inlay portrait of Nefertiti.

39. A royal inlay head with edge carving prepared for the addition of a crown and features in other materials. (H. 9 cm.).

In the King's portrait, facing left, the surface abrasion partly masks the light modelling of the face which is faintly coloured with flesh-coloured paint, and the lips with light red. Although unfinished, the profile carving is carried round the front edge, suggesting the possibility of another raised inlay; it is shaped in much the same way as on a glass head for inlay. On the nose and lips, the dark paint guide-lines have not yet been cut away; these also remain in the eye and eyebrow recesses being prepared for separate inlays. The head is shaped for the addition of a separate crown; the lobe of the ear is pierced. The cheek is firm, but it is raised to reflect the beginning of the smile shown by a line at the corner of the mouth; the jaw-line is masculine compared with the other inlay.

Woolley found inlay portraits of the King and Queen in the chapel at Maruaten, one of which, now in the Ashmolean Museum, has rounded-edge carving similar to the King's profile.

Plate 45

[UC 102 and 101]
Provenance: Amarna. Yellow quartzite. Height of broken fragment 6·0 cm. Width 6·5 cm. (102). Height of King's inlay 9·0 cm. Width 9·0 cm. (101). Lit. J. Samson, *C/A III*, text, p. 226, pl. CV (4 and 7). Comparisons: C. L. Woolley, *C/A I*, p. 121, pl. XXXV (1 and 2), London, 1923; Ashmolean, No. 1922 (95).

40. A royal inlay with delicately carved face prepared for an inlaid eye and eyebrow and the addition of a crown. (H. 10 cm.).

[UC 103]

Provenance: Amarna. Yellow quartzite. Height 10·0 cm. Width 11·0 cm. Width across back 10·0 cm. Depth 6·0 cm. Lit. J. Samson, *C/A III*, text, p. 226, pl. CV. Comparisons: [1]Head of Smenkhkare, J. D. S. Pendlebury, *C/A III*, p. 12 (33/6), pl. LIX (6–8). Brooklyn inlay, 33.685.

Much of the quality of this inlay is lost in a photograph. The warm tan-coloured stone has been worked to a marble-smoothness and the planes of the face are so subtly carved that only by handling it can its full textural finish be appreciated. The profile faces left. It has a sharp edge and was evidently intended to be deeply set into a wall so that the face was flush with the surface. The ear is well carved and the lobe shown as pierced.

The eye socket and eyebrow are prepared for inlays and the head for a crown, with possibly a streamer inlaid in the triangular groove behind the ear. Such detail shows that the robes and regalia were added to some of the carefully wrought royal inlays at Amarna, making them composite figures like those inlaid on Tutankhamen's golden throne.

The lips which are painted red appear to have been lifted in a smile; they are not the full drooping feature familiar on many portraits of Akhenaten, Nefertiti, Ty and Tutankhamen. The features seem to have been shallower than Akhenaten's and the expression of resigned sweetness more characteristic of the statue head from the Great Temple, in the Brooklyn Museum and the inlay head in that Museum.[1]

VI. *Fragments of faience tiles and inlays of fruit, flowers and from figures. Mosaic fragments in the bottom row. (Tallest H. 7 cm.).*

VII. *Coloured faience tiles, a duck, fish and reeds from pool scenes. (Tallest H. 7·9 cm.).*

VIII. *Moulds, with relevant faience objects made in them or similar examples. (Triangular mould H. 6·6 cm.).*

69

Coarse, very white limestone has been used for this head which faces right and is carved with a flat back for inlaying. The negroid characteristics of a prognathous jaw, thick lips, high cheek bones and a receding forehead are well observed and technical skill has been combined with artistic insight, in the carving. It is not a flat profile. The nose and lips are just turned around the edge giving a depth that is enhanced by the modelling of the eyebrow, the bridge of the nose and the shapely jaw line. These details, with the varied planes in the face, the wig and the typical ear-ring animate this head, which would have had significance even in a large wall scene.

To fit it well into the background, the tip of the nose and the end of the chin have been squared. As a non-royal portrait it is not carved to receive additional inlaid details in faience, stones or glass, as are the royal heads.

[UC 009]
Provenance: Amarna. Coarse limestone. Height 8·0 cm. Width 8·0 cm. Lit. J. Samson, *C/A III*, text, p. 227, pl. CVI (4).

41. Deeply carved non-royal head for inlay without preparation for additional features. (H. 8 cm.).

AN 'AMARNA' PRINCESS FROM THEBES

This small gilded wooden figure comes from Qurneh, near the Theban valley of the Tombs of the Kings, and in 1927, five years after Tutankhamen's tomb had been excavated there, Petrie wrote that it was "probably a daughter of Akhenaten".[1] Further study of it in comparison with details on some of Tutankhamen's furniture from his tomb strengthens this probability, and by its comparison with other figures, suggests that the youngest Amarna princesses went to live with Tutankhamen and his Queen, their older sister,

70

42. *The figure of Tutankhamen and Queen Ankhesenamen are carved and painted on this ivory lid and below them two royal ladies, probably the Queen's younger sisters, pick mandrakes in a garden.*

Facsimile of Colour Plate IV. See p.64.

after their parents died and the Court eventually returned to Thebes under Tutankhamen.

The small standing figure faces left. It is made of wood, coated with gesso and covered with gold in the manner of a number of Tutankhamen's small figures. The face is finely carved in profile; the well-cut chin can be seen in detail where the gold has worn off. The body is slender with shoulders shown frontally, but the hips, and the legs which are only carved to the knees, turn towards the left. The left arm of the figure is bent across the body, as in numbers of the princesses' figures, and here holds a cornet-shaped bouquet sheath over the left shoulder. The upper right arm is beside the body but then reaches out from the skirt, as though holding something. The hand is missing and was evidently carved with whatever it held, because except for a splinter of raw reddish wood projecting from the top of the head and

43. Sketch of a wooden box lid from Tutankhamen's tomb with kilt on Amarna princess resembling the figures on plate 42 (Cairo).

[UC 24311]
Provenance: Qurneh, West Bank, Thebes; Amarna or Post-Amarna Period, *c.* 1379-1352 B.C. Wood, coated with *gesso* and gold. Height 7·3 cm. Width 3·0 cm. Lit. [1]W. M F. Petrie, *Objects of Daily Use*, p. 43 pl. XXXVIII (29), 1927. Comparisons: [2]H. Carter and A. C. Mace, *Tomb of Tutankhamen*, 1923-1933, Vol. I, pl. LXIII; [3]Vol. III, frontispiece; [4]Vol. III, p. 118; [5]It is worn by the small figure picking grapes on an ivory plaque in the Louvre (E.14,374), C. Desroches-Noblecourt, J.E.A. 54, pl. XIV, 1968; [6]C. Desroches-Noblecourt, *Tutankhamen*, p. 244, fig. 148, London, 1967.

obviously broken from the background, all the edges—at the wrist, top of the head and sheath, and at the knees—appear to have been finished; in most places where the gold has worn off, there are the remains of the white gesso under-coat. These surfaces were presumably fitted against other objects in an openwork or inlaid scene, as on much of Tutankhamen's furniture. Possibly lotuses were placed at the top of the sheath and perhaps a "sash", by the right hand. The piece is backed by a finely woven material under a red substance, probably adhesive (?).

The wig on this gold figure, although without the uraeus, is the same shape as worn by the Queen on the back of Tutankhamen's golden throne.[2] In itself this is no proof of the identity or sex of the epicene little figure; comparing it with others on an ivory lid from Tutankhamen's tomb shows it is not possible to determine people's sex in this period by what they wear.[3]

On the ivory lid, it is the King who wears a similar wig. He and the Queen stand facing each other above two small kneeling figures, picking flowers in a garden, described by Howard Carter as "Court maidens".[4] But one wears the wig, with a fillet, as this gold figure and the King above; she carries in her bent left arm a sheaf of flowers over her left shoulder. The other wears the long plaited wig, with the royal side-lock like the Queen above her. Both kneeling figures wear the *shendyt* kilt like the King, normally worn by men,[5] but there is a parallel for a princess wearing it on another box from the tomb, where Nefer-neferu-re, the second youngest princess, wears the same kilt.[6] Her named portrait, the small figures on the ivory lid, and this gold figure have enough likenesses and features in common to indicate that they are probably all portraits of the youngest Amarna princesses at the Theban Court.

There is no data as to where at Qurneh the gold figure came from. Scattered in the area around Tutankhamen's tomb were objects bearing his name; a bowl in the desert, and gold, with his name and that of Ankhesenamen and Ay on it in a rock-hewn chamber. Embalmers' equipment was found in the pit, with the flower necklace from a guest at the funeral banquet. This figure, too, could be an object from his Court; it has the *insouciant* grace of the young royal figures of the Amarna age.

[UC 1. 314; 2. 295; 3. 316; 4. 304/312; 5. 296; 6. 310; 7. 260; 8. 326; 9. 122; 10. 128; 11. 271; 12. 123; 13. 263/64; 14. 194; 15. 307; 16. 279; 17. 24524; 18. 288; 19. 273; 20-22. 281/286/680] Provenance: Amarna. Limestone, sandstone, slate, quartzite, marble, diorite, a porous "pumice stone" and Egyptian alabaster, usually applied to calcite in Egyptian antiquities. The tall white reed, top centre. Height 11·5 cm. Width 3·5 cm. The small black reed, right of centre, bottom row. Height 3·5 cm. Width 0·5 cm. Lit. [1]P. *T/A*, pp. 11, 12. Unpublished.

STONE INLAYS

On this plate are some of the many stone inlays which Petrie found; these had fallen from the walls, cornices and doorways of the buildings at Amarna which were destroyed and quarried for stone. They repeat in a variety of colours the glazed inlays which he described and drew in detail.[1] Limestone, he notes, was a favourite background for the inlays, which is understandable in view of the marble-smooth white surface they gave the finest pieces, which must have gleamed in the sunlight and made the multi-coloured inscriptions legible, and the scenes visible from afar. Red and black granite and diorite inlaid in the white background, black granite in yellow quartzite, white alabaster in red granite were some of the examples he found. The skill in carving the brittle stones was consummate. In small inscriptions, glass and obsidian were used for the slim lines, of which there are some examples in the Collection.

Bottom Row

In the bottom row, except for the smaller slate example of the wick of flax, ḥ[1], on the left of the central disk,[2] all the signs are of diorite; left is the goddess M3't,[3] and the larger ḥ sign;[4] in the centre, the disk is over the knot of rope from the base of a cartouche;[5] on the right of that is the reed sign;[6] the dark fragment second to the right has spaces for inlaid leaves (?), presumably of another colour,[7] and in the bottom right corner is a bunch of grapes,[8] more usually found in the bright blue glaze.

In the centre row, the fingers on the left,[9] and the hand from an inlaid figure[10] are of limestone and quartzite respectively. The disk and horns are limestone;[11] the beautifully carved foot from an inlaid figure is of quartzite[12] and the feet of a wader bird of sandstone.[13] On the left, above the fingers, are two slate claws (?), remaining inlaid in a porous pumice-like stone[14] and in the top left corner, the water sign is also slate.[15] The broken feather on its right is a slate-like stone,[16] and below it, the geometric sign is marble.[17] The large central reed is Egyptian alabaster,[18] like the broken shape in the top right corner which is perhaps the calyx of a large lotus design.[19] The cluster of three[20]–[22] small inlays between them are all of marble.

44. A variety of stone inlays from figures and hieroglyphic inscriptions. (H. 11·5 cm. to 3·5 cm.).

73

Glass

Facsimile of Colour Plate V. See p. 64.

[UC 2235]
Provenance: Unknown. Amarna period. Opaque red (cuprous oxide) glass. Height 9·0 cm. Width 4·5 cm. Lit. J. Samson, *C/A III*, p. 228, pl. CVII (4). Comparisons: [1]P. *T/A*, pp. 25-27. Mural, Ashmolean Museum, Oxford, No. 1893.1. See, N. de G. Davies, *J.E.A.*, VII, frontispiece.

Plate 14b

AMARNA PRINCESSES—RED MOULDED GLASS

Besides the technical interest of this early piece of glass moulded for inlay, its artistry has achieved a notable portrait of two of the Amarna princesses as children. They face right and their nude figures with arms around each other's shoulders convey their youthfulness. The left arm of the taller princess is missing and the legs are broken off at the knees.

As the piece is not included in Petrie's description of glass-making at Amarna, it is undoubtedly a more recent acquisition! He wrote of polished glass, cut mouldings and engraved patterns and, in some unpublished notes, of glass being patted into strips for inlays and small figures; all these processes are evident in this piece. Its flat back and straight sides were apparently shaped in a mould, but the curves of the faces and bodies were probably modelled by hand. Narrow ribbon strips appear to have been applied for the princesses' hands on each other's shoulders and for their ears; the ear of the taller princess has a scratch in front of it from a tool (?). Delicate lines made within the forms, to finish shaping the bodies, were evidently engraved with a sharp edged tool while the material was still viscid.

A break across the middle of the figures has been joined and the original red of the glass can be seen in the fractures of the piece which is otherwise covered by a "bloom". Otherwise discolouration is limited to small patches of blue-black on the sides and back.

The delicacy of the inlay resembles the red glass figures of Tutankhamen and Ankhesenamen inlaid on the back of his golden throne, and it possibly came from a similarly elaborate scene. In sensitivity it is reminiscent of the Amarna princesses as children at the feet of their parents, in the Ashmolean mural from their house, and possibly it was part of a similar family group.

SIX OBJECTS OF 'AMARNA' GLASS

In this plate of glass objects, the head and the three hieroglyphs (top left, centre and bottom right) are inlays; the pair at the top right are red ear-rings and the fragment at the bottom left is from a glass vessel.

1. *Hieroglyph ḥ, (i) left:*

The wick of twisted flax is dark blue glass which can be seen dark and shiny in a crack at the side of it. Otherwise the front and particularly the less polished back has a "bloom" on it which also covers the break at the top and

[UC 302]
Provenance: Amarna. Glass. Height 5·0 cm. Width 1·5 cm. Unpublished.

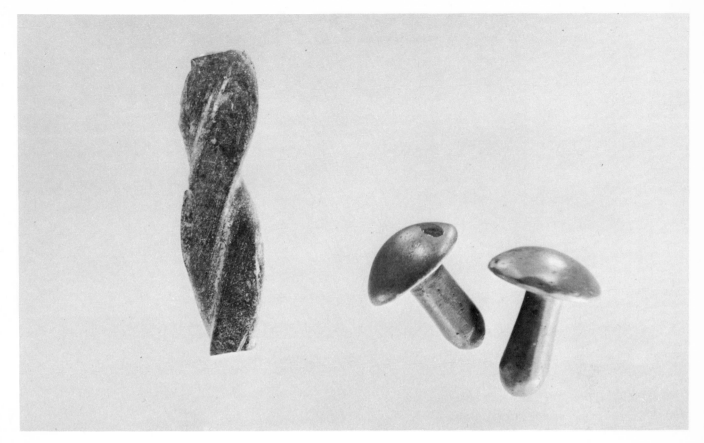

bottom of the piece. It is an inlay with a flat back and shallow straight sides probably moulded. The twists of flax could have been applied in strips or may possibly have been shaped and·divided by a tool while the glass was viscid.

2. *Red glass ear-rings, (i) right:*

The pair of opaque red (cuprous oxide) stud ear-rings show no sign of a join between the stud and the shank. The glass has only the faintest surface "bloom" which pales the colour and presumably, if there were a chip, the fuller brownish red would show underneath. The only evidence of decay besides the "bloom" is occasional faint green veining perceptible on the studs. There is no possibility, in this example, of the thick shank being attached to the stud by a thinner screw which could go more comfortably through a pierced ear-lobe; the shanks are approximately 0·8 centimetres in diameter near the end which is shaped (squeezed?) into a rough point.

3. *Inlay head, (ii) top left:*

This remarkable inlay is of opaque red glass as can be seen in a small chip; otherwise the surface has decayed to an opaque chalky irridescence of pink and green. The piece has the flat back and straight upright sides of moulded glass; the back is roughened as though to help fix it to the background. The depth of the edge of the profile is 0·5 centimetres.

The inlay faces right. The eye and a line of the eyebrow are recessed for additional inlays. The line from the brow to the tip of the nose is at the angle usual in the princesses' profiles. The nostril is delicately modelled and at the inner corner of the mouth is the downward line seen in many Amarna portraits. The lips are thick, and they and the line between them, as well as the shape of the chin, are carried around the side as though to fit into a

45(i). Glass hieroglyph (H. 5 cm.) and red ear-rings.

[UC 22881]
Provenance: Amarna. Glass. Diameter of studs 2·0 cm. Length of shank 1·7 cm. Diameter 0·8 cm. Lit. J. Samson, *C/A III*, p. 228.

[UC 22078]
Provenance: Unknown. Amarna style. Glass. Height 3·1 cm. Width 2·8 cm. Depth 0·6 cm. across the neck. Unpublished. Comparisons: E. Rief-stahl, *AEG & G.*, Nos. 43 and 76, Brooklyn, 1969. H. Muller, *AKK & MAS*, p. 95, A 135.

75

precise outline prepared for the inlay. The nostril is only modelled on the surface. The modelling on the face would have risen from the background in *bas-relief*, with the head evidently meant to be placed into the background.

Up the back of the neck and face runs a thin vertical raised line to meet another raised line on a downward angle at the top of the face where the head-dress would be placed. The area between the raised lines is recessed. Two incised lines in the neck show the typical Amarna folds.

The head and features are in the mature style of Amarna art. A composite inlay in glass made with such delicacy and precision suggests a royal head from a figure like those of Tutankhamen and his Queen on the back of his golden throne. Its appearance suggests an Amarna princess, perhaps from such a scene on royal furniture.

Plate 14b

45(ii). Inlay head (H. 3·1 cm.), hieroglyphs and fragment of bowl.

[UC 305]
Provenance: Amarna. Glass. Length 2·2 cm. Width 0·5 cm. Unpublished.

[UC 12476]
Provenance: Amarna. Glass. Height 3·0 cm. Diameter 5·6 cm. Lit. P. *T/A*, pl. XIII, 36. W. M. F. Petrie, *Scarabs and Cylinders*, pl. XXXVI, 18, 10. (51), London, 1917.

[UC 289]
Provenance: Amarna. Glass. Height 2·2 cm. Width 4·4 cm. Unpublished. Comparison: P. *T/A*, pp. 25–28, pl. XIIİ.

4. *The N sign, (ii) top right:*
Part of the hieroglyph *n* is broken at both ends. It is opaque dark blue-black glass, now misted over with a "bloom" except in the fractures where the original dark depth of the colour shows.

5. *Fragment of blue glass vessel, (ii) bottom left:*
The opaque blue glass of this convex fragment from a vessel is completely covered by pale brown decay except for some chips around the broken edges where the light, bright blue shows. Inlaid white remains in the hieroglyphs of the earlier name of the Aten in the top part of two cartouches. On the left cartouche is *m rn.f m Šw n* (. . . .); on the right *Ḥr 3ḫt* (. . . .).

6. *Inlay hieroglyph, the sun's rays, (ii) bottom right:*
The surface of this opaque dark blue glass inlay is now covered by a pale chalky "bloom". It is part of the hieroglyph *ḥr*. The incised lines across the "hill" and forming the sun's rays are uneven, little more than scratched on, presumably when the glass was viscid.

76

Faience and Moulds

FAIENCE OBJECTS FROM THE COLLECTION

The term "faience" in this context is used to describe objects from Amarna made of quartz frit (powdered quartz) and then glazed. The few examples from the Collection shown here include separate inlays, glazed tiles with inlaid designs, amulets and seals.

Some fit into or closely resemble examples in the thousands of moulds brought back by Petrie from Amarna. Others show variations on the Amarna themes.

ANIMAL AMULETS AND RINGS

All thirty-three objects in these plates are faience animals, felines, birds, fish, reptiles and insects. The majority are amulets with threading holes intact or fragmentary; the second row are all ring bezels; and some, particularly the hieroglyphs, are inlays. Those without a reference to Petrie's publication *Tell el-Amarna* are unpublished.

"Cats" (i)

In the first row are "cats", large and small. On the extreme left, the seated cat has an intact threading hole fitted into the hollow at the back of the head. It is carved identically on both sides and was glazed back and front, but most of the colour has faded and worn to patches of pale green with the white composition showing between them. The cat facing right is seated on a base. The pose, upright ears and mask are typically feline.

Lit. P. *T/A*, chap. II, p. 12; chap. IV, pp. 25-30, pls. XVI-XX. J. Samson, *C/A III*, pp. 228/229; pls. CVII (5-10); pl. CVIII (UC 2115, 1147, 1238, 1360, 722, 1258, 2038, 1106, 1114). Comparisons: *C/A*, Pt. I, II and III. E. Riefstahl, *Glass and Glazes from Ancient Egypt*, Brooklyn Museum, 1948 and *Ancient Egyptian Glass and Glazes*, Brooklyn Museum, 1969. H. W. Muller, *Agyptische Kunstwerde, Kleinfunde und Glas*, Berlin, 1964. A. Lucas, *Ancient Egyptian Materials and Industries* (4th edition revised by J. R. Harris), London, 1962.

[UC 23979]
Height 2·0 cm. Width 1·2 cm.

46(i). Faience "Cats".

To the right of it are three amulets of small indistinctly modelled, seated cats. Their bodies face right on a thin base, but their heads turn to the front. The threading hole is through the body of the central example and on the back of the right-hand cat, but broken. They are glazed front and back,

[UC 23689, 1213, 23680]
Height 0·8 cm.

blue, yellow and blue-green in that order. They are so small and roughly made that their significance may have been merely as pet kittens for children's amulets.

[UC 1189]
Length 1·0 cm.

The animal second from the right is blurred by the covering of white glaze. It appears to be stalking on all fours, moving to the right. A fragment at the back is possibly part of a threading hole.

[UC 1211]
Height 1·8 cm. Width 0·6 cm.

In the top right corner is a back view of a distinctly made figure of the goddess Sekhmet. It is glazed bright blue. The lioness-headed human figure faces forward and stands on a base. It is finely made. The ears are upright on the leonine head. Over the breasts are the lappets of a wig. The right arm hangs by the side, the left bends forward over the body to hold a papyrus sceptre to the front. There is a threading hole through the head. On the back are two parallel horizontal ridges shown on the plate.

46(ii). Ring bezels and fish amulets.
(Tallest 1·7 cm.)

First Row (ii)

In the first row all the objects are ring bezels with remnants of the shanks behind. All the animals face right, except the calf in the broken bezel second to the right.

[UC 1030]
Diam. 1·5 cm. Lit. P. *T/A*, pl. XVI (185).

The bezel on the left is glazed yellow on both sides; it is oval with broken ends. The open-work design shows a frisking calf in the reeds, which Petrie noted was in the jewellery as well as on the painted floors in the central palace. The bovid has large ears and it gallops to the right with tail arched. A double line makes a feature of the rim.

[UC 23814]
Height 1·7 cm.

Next to it is the left side of an unusually deep broken bezel in apple green glaze. On it, a long-horned ibex (?) with a powerful neck, upright head and large curled horns is finely executed. Below it is a calf resting on one knee with the other raised; it faces left and it is apparently a suckling, taking its mother's milk. It has long ears, an upturned stump of a tail and the leggy gawkiness of a young animal.

[UC 1026]
Length 2·0 cm.

The centre bezel is a bright blue oval with straight ends. It is glazed blue both sides but the back, where the shank joined the bezel, is touched with brown. A long-horned ibex (?) prances right with lifted forelegs and the hind legs separated as though it were moving. The tail is short; the surrounding reeds are blurred.

[UC 2038]
Length 1·5 cm.

The broken bezel second right is glazed olive green both sides. In the open-work design a long-horned ibex (?) is lying with its legs bent under it.

The carving is perfectly formed in *bas-relief*, the horns carved well, in front of the notched top rim, and the flowing lines of the animal are unspoilt by the break in the bezel behind it.

On the left, the bezel which is straight at both ends and perhaps meant to be at the top, is glazed yellow both sides. The ibex has long curved horns and a stumpy tail. The legs are bent and the rump of the animal raised as though it were moving fast. Below it is a shape of reeds (?).

Second Row

Of the fish in this row, two are amulets, one probably an inlay, and two are probably ring bezels.

On the left, the fish facing right is bright blue and glazed both sides. It is slightly convex and, although without the signs of a shank, was probably intended for a small ring bezel. It is very similar to the one on the right of the row which was thus intended. It resembles the '*int* or "bulti" fish. The head, tail and fins are shaped, and the nose, eyes and gills are incised. Petrie has a similar mould on Plate XVII (331) T/A.

Second on the left, the largest fish with the head missing is glazed white on the front and flat back and was possibly an inlay. The body is slightly convex on the obverse. The scales are stippled and the fins and tail striped. Two upward-curving lines are incised along the lower body from the break. The details are well executed.

The two slim fish resemble the *ḥ3t* of the Oxyrhynchus fish, and are both amulets. The centre one is glazed in bright blue all round, with the nose, fins and tail shaped and an intact threading hole at the head. The second example from the right is covered with faded pale blue glaze. The features of the fish are similar but less well defined. The threading hole on the nose is broken. Both are shown upside down. The "bulti"-type fish on the right is blue and resembles the one on the left of the row, but the features are blurred by poor glazing. It is definitely a ring bezel with traces of the shanks remaining. The head, tail and fins are shaped, the eye incised as a circle behind the nose. The body is striped and stippled.

[UC 2036]
Length 1·8 cm. P. *T/A*, pl. XVI (188).

[UC 1180]
Length 2·0 cm.

[UC 2061]
Length 2·4 cm. Width 2·0 cm.

Similar mould, P. *T/A*, pl. XVII (330)

[UC 2064, 1179]
Fish 1. Length 1·9 cm. Fish 2. Length 2·0 cm. P. *T/A*, pl. XVI (195).

Comparison: P. *T/A*, pl. XVII (332).

46(iii). Faience birds. (Tallest 1·5 cm.)

Birds (iii)

Left of the row above, with faded blue glaze on all surfaces is an amulet of the Horus falcon, facing right. It is characteristically shaped front and back. The wing feathers descend to the tail which rests on the base, as do the front legs; these are defined on both sides and a hole separates them from the body. The threading hole behind the head is intact.

Second left, the bird has worn green glaze on the front and flat back. The strong neck, long low body and sturdy legs suggest a duck or goose. The end tail feathers are missing, but it might be a white-fronted *gb*-goose from an inlaid inscription. It faces right; lines distinguish the wings and the legs.

Third left, the long-legged heron has green glaze both sides. It has the

[UC 23674]
Height 1·5 cm. Width 1·5 cm.
Similar mould, P. *T/A*, pl. XVII (314).

[UC 1215]
Length 1·3 cm. Height 1·5 cm.

[UC 1214]
Height 1·4 cm.

[UC 2122]
Length 2·0 cm.

[UC 2121]
Wing span 2·0 cm. Length 1·5 cm.

[UC 1064]
Length 1·8 cm. Height 1·0 cm.

[UC 1173]
Height 1·5 cm. Width 0·9 cm.

[UC 1171]
Height 1·5 cm. Width 0·6 cm.

[UC 1169]
Height 2·3 cm. Width 0·9 cm.

head and crest, curved neck, body feathers and straight legs of the *šnty* heron and although so delicately made, may have been from an inscription. It also resembles the *bnw* phoenix. The eye is incised; the bird, facing right, stands on a base.

Third from the right, the bird is glazed green on the front and flat back, and it faces right. It was possibly the hieroglyph *wr* from an inscription, as it resembles the swallow or martin with the squared tail feathers. The glaze is worn on the front surface but shapes the wings and tail. The legs are bent and placed on a short base.

The flying bird second from the right is glazed on the front and flat back with a pale red. The head has a small blob on it but this is unlikely to be a threading hole and the piece was probably an inlay. The spread wings are striped with feathers, also suggested on the body and tail.

The ring bezel on the right has a worn blue glaze on all surfaces. A bird is fixed in an upright position in the centre, possibly a roughly shaped chick. There are traces at the back where the shank has broken off both sides. The raised shape fixed at right angles to the bezel must have made a clumsy ring and it is remarkable that such a frail fixture has remained in place.

Top Row (iv)

In the top row are six examples of the cobra, all of which had threading holes and are presumably amulets.

On the left, covered by a "peacock" or green-blue glaze, is a cobra with head and puffed neck, which is raised; the rest of the body is curled in horizontal rings behind it on a base. It faces right and the projection from the head is an intact threading hole.

Second left, the cobra is covered with a faded green glaze. It faces frontally. Down the body are raised V-shapes like the cloisons on ornate jewelled uraei.

Third left, the raised head and puffed-out neck of the cobra are in the same position. There was a threading hole at the back, now broken, and the green glaze covering the piece is faded. Below the head are the V-shaped cloisons of larger bejewelled examples. They are in the position of Akhenaten's name on the mould, left of the third row on Plate 49, which this faience amulet otherwise resembles. The head, eyes and mouth are distinctly modelled.

46(iv). Reptiles and insects. (Tallest 2·3 cm.)

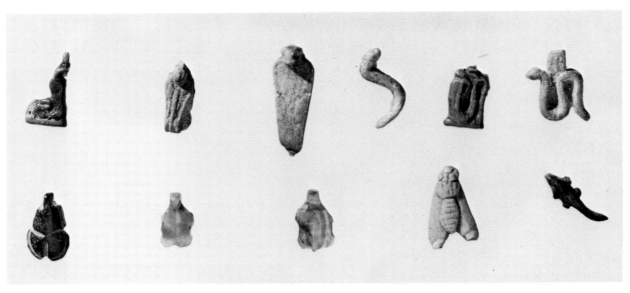

80

Third from the right is an amulet of a twisting snake, glazed blue all over. The body is puffed-out below the head, but thins as it descends and twists back on itself. The eye is clearly marked. There is a broken threading hole behind the head.

[UC 2148]
Length 1·5 cm. Width 0·6 cm.

In both the last two amulets on the right, the cobra has its head raised and body undulating against a background. Second from the right, the snake and background are glazed blue all over. The raised head and puffed-out body drops and then curls up and down on a base line and against the background from which there was a threading hole in the top, centre.

[UC 1921]
Height 1·3 cm. Width 0·8 cm.

On the extreme right, the snake covered in faded green glass is in the same undulating position but the head is pushed forward and the body is not puffed out. The background is smaller and there is no base line. The threading hole at the top is intact.

[UC 23644]
Height 1·5 cm. Width 1·2 cm.

Second Row

In the next row are four flies in different colours and materials, and on the right a small faience lizard. On the left is a black stone fly, well shaped, with a broken threading hole from its head.

[UC 1197]
Height 1·5 cm. Width 1·0 cm.

The next two flies are well carved in carnelian and are very similar. The first has a complete threading hole from its head.

[UC 23664]
Length 1·2 cm. Width 0·7 cm.

In the one in the centre of the plate, the threading hole is broken.

[UC 23829]
Length 1·1 cm. Width 0·7 cm.

Second to the right, the fly amulet is glazed all over in pale red. The carving is detailed. The eyes bulge from the head, which, like the body, is striped. The wings are well modelled.

[UC 2132]
Length 1·7 cm. Width 1·1 cm.

In the right corner, the faience lizard amulet is glazed green all over. It is shaped as the *ḥnt3sw*, perhaps for *'s3*—"many". From the long tapering body with the tail swung to one side, two legs are shown each side and the distinctly shaped head has a threading hole through it.

[UC 1187]
Length 1·6 cm. Width 0·5 cm.

ROYAL AND RELIGIOUS FAIENCE AMULETS

The faience amulets in these plates show the retention of old ideas and beliefs by the people of Amarna where these amulets were made for them to wear. Few of them relate directly to Aten worship.

The amulet on the left below and next to it on the right are both crouching figures in the traditionally infantile pose of finger to mouth as shown in moulds in the middle row, Plate 49. Hayes thought these represented the King as a child of the Aten.[1] But the appearance of the left example is more like the traditional figure of the infant Horus, although the blue one on its right is unmistakably the King.

47(i). Symbolic figures. (Tallest 3·3 cm.)

[UC 1239]
Height 3·3 cm. Depth 0·5 cm.

[UC 1240]
Height 2·3 cm. Width 1·0 cm.

[UC 2008]
Height 2·0 cm. Width 1·0 cm.

[UC 1221]
Height 2·0 cm. Width 18·0 cm.

[UC 997, 2009]
Diam. at back 1·5 cm. Width 1·0 cm.

[UC 1247, 1244]
Height 1·5 cm. Width 0·7 cm.

[UC 1103]
Length 2·5 cm. Width 0·9 cm.

[UC 1377]
Height 2·2 cm.

[UC 1376]
Height 2·0 cm.

The larger example is glazed red overall and has an intact threading hole from the head. The figure is seated on a base, facing right with right hand on knee and left to lips. The glaze by the neck is blurred but appears to fall from the head in the side-lock worn by the infant Horus.

Second from the left the crouching figure of the King, hand to mouth, faces right. He wears the blue crown with a streamer down the back and the *shendyt* kilt. The amulet is glazed blue overall and the threading hole from the top of the head is intact. Hayes wrote of these openwork figures in the Metropolitan Museum as being only blue,[1] but there is a similar one in the Ashmolean Museum which is yellow glaze.

Third from the left the small, comparatively indistinct figure has a worn blue glaze, overall. The figure faces right with profile face and feet and frontal body. On the head is possibly a plumed head-dress, as the top projection is a broken threading hole; it has a leonine appearance, perhaps a mane, and the figure could be Bes, one of the most popular Amarna amulets, with left hand forward holding a gnarled stick and the right one behind him bending to his tail.

Fourth from the left, the small figure stands on a base against a background and faces right. It is covered with a blurred, pale blue glass-like glaze. The shape suggests a bearded King wearing the Crown of Lower Egypt and a kilt is suggested. The left hand holds a sceptre (?) in front; the right hangs down the back.

The two ovals third and fourth from the right are ring bezels with the remains of shanks behind them. The blurred design of the left example is explained by the one on its right. That on the left is glazed blue all over. In the openwork design, a small figure faces a tall shape on the right which it touches with the left hand, the right arm dropping behind the figure. The design is too indistinct to be self explanatory but interesting to compare with the parallel scene on the right. This bezel is glazed green back and front and has part of the shank remaining one side. In this the figure appears to be the Queen in a tall crown and either a clinging gown, or none, standing in the same pose in relation to a high floral decoration in a garden or perhaps a pavilion, as there are shapes hanging above, resembling bunches of grapes. The same overhead decor is on the plaque on the bottom right corner. The top edge of the green bezel is broken. Both bezels are the same size and were probably children's rings.

The last two amulets in the top row are both small naked figures striding to the right, against a background. On both the overall green glaze has faded. Both have an arm hanging before and behind the figure. There is a blurred wig (?) on the back of the heads.

First Row (ii)

Left of the first row, covered in dark, matt, purple glaze is the *tit*-amulet, found with those signifying life and welfare and sometimes connected with Isis. As they are often red, the glaze on this one has possibly darkened. It is chipped at the top but has an intact threading hole at the bottom.

The larger *ḥst*-vase third from the left is glazed bright blue and has the remains of a threading hole from the bottom, with possibly another at the top.

The smaller *ḥst*-vase in the centre is a dark purple vitreous glaze with

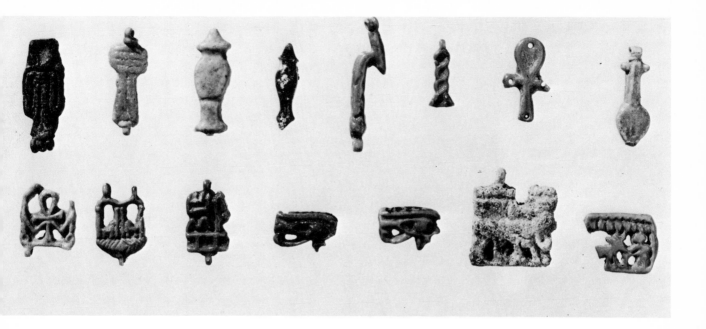

faint pink showing in the irridescent surface. It has the remains of a threading hole top and bottom.

The *w3s*-sceptre is glazed bright blue overall and has a complete threading hole top and bottom.

Third from the right the wick of flax is glazed blue, overall, and has an intact threading hole at the top.

The *ʿankh* sign second from the right is glazed bright blue overall. Four threading holes were pierced through it front to back at the top, bottom and on both sides; the right hand one is now broken away.

The *nfr* sign on the right is completely glazed with blue, now faded. A threading hole remains at the top with a trace left of one at the bottom.

Bottom Row

Left of the bottom row is the *ʿankh* with arms both sides holding the edges of an enclosing *ḥb-sd* booth (?). This is broken at the top right corner. The amulet is glazed blue at front and back. One threading hole is intact in the bottom left-hand corner with the suggestion of the remains of another on the right and possibly one at the break on the left side.

Second left of the bottom row the *ḥb-sd* festival hall is glazed blue overall, with two complete threading holes at the top and a broken one at the centre bottom. The design is clear and detailed and has the diamond shape in the semi-circular base.

Third left and glazed blue overall is the phrase *mry 'Imn*. The hieroglyphs are against a background and, although an unexpected amulet for Amarna, it has a complete threading hole top and bottom.

Two of the very numerous *wḏ3t* eyes in the centre of the bottom row are both glazed blue overall. The one on the left has a *nfr* sign on the back; the other an *ʿankh*.

Second from the right, the amulet which is almost square is grey and gritty in texture, possibly unglazed. A bovine animal wearing plumes on its head is festooned as those shown in procession, possibly to be sacrificed for an Aten altar.[2] It is walking to the right. With the top threading hole, which is intact, it is perhaps a cow or bull with amuletic significance.

47(ii). Hieroglyphic amulets. (Tallest 3 cm.)

[UC 2102]
Length 3·0 cm.

[UC 1112]
Length 1·4 cm.

[UC 2093]
Length 1·8 cm.

[UC 1110]
Length 2·2 cm.

[UC 1108]
Length 1·5 cm. Width 1·2 cm.

[UC 1113]
Length 1·8 cm. Width 1·1 cm.

[UC 1107]
Length 1·9 cm. Width 0·9 cm.

[UC 24208, 1151]
Length 1·4 cm. and 1·5 cm.

[UC 2142]
Height 2·0 cm. Width 2·7 cm.

[UC 1016]
Width 1·5 cm. Height 1·3 cm.
Comparisons: [1]W. C. Hayes, *Scepter of Egypt*, II, pp. 290-291, New York, 1968; [2]N. de G. Davies, *RTA*, I, pl. XIV, London, 1903; [3]J. D. Cooney, *Amarna Reliefs from Hermopolis in American Collections*, Nos. 38 and 39, Brooklyn Museum, 1965. G. Roeder, *Amarna Reliefs aus Hermopolis*, pl. 175, pl. 33, Hildesheim, 1969.

On the bottom right corner is a rectangular plaque broken at the left. It is glazed blue front and back, although, at the back, a horizontal strip across the centre remains unglazed, as though it had been mounted on a cross-bar. No trace of threading hole or shank remains. It resembles a scene in a manger, or perhaps a shrine. Facing right is the front of the body, the forelegs and head of a calf-like animal with large ears, a horn and long head. On its right facing it, a small standing figure reaches towards its mouth as though feeding it. Across the top of the enclosure is a row of decoration, apparently suspended (bunches of grapes?), which are met by points from a serrated edge at the top of the plaque; the right and bottom rims are plain. The open-work design is carefully wrought and placed, and although the feeding of a bovine animal in a manger is shown in Amarna reliefs from Hermopolis,[3] the decoration of this suggests a royal or religious enclosure.

FAIENCE SEALS

At the top of the plate are two half cylinder seals, either unfinished, or with the other half of each broken away. The outside of both is covered with a purple glaze not continued inside.

See Plate 50, top right mould

[UC 2031]
Length 2·0 cm. P. *T/A*, pl. XVI (182).

The horizontal open-work design on the left has a single rounded rim each end, from a mould. The design is horizontal; one bovine creature leaps to the right with head turned backwards and tail curled forward. Beneath it is a smaller, calf-like animal which springs to the left with tail outstretched. Petrie noted the parallel with the leaping calves on the palace painted pavements. Between and around the creatures is open-work design, strengthened by more solid shapes in the faience above and in front of the larger animal, but the piece is relatively fragile and possibly more decorative than useful.

[UC 2032]
Height 2·5 cm. P. *T/A*, pl. XVI (183).

The vertical seal on the right, also of violet glaze, is solid. There are three rounded rims at the top and two at the bottom edge. The vertical design is of a standing crowned god or king-like figure with a tall head-dress and skirt to the knees. His right hand is raised at the back of his head. He faces right and his left hand reaches out in front, perhaps to hold a sceptre or perhaps to touch an upright structure, possibly a tree (?). In front of this, the designs are more difficult to interpret but could be of an ibex below and perhaps a symbolic bird above. The design is not typically Egyptian in feeling and suggests Asiatic influence.

The three scarabs in the second row and the four frogs beneath them are all seals with longitudinal threading holes.

[UC 23662]
Length 1·6 cm.

On the left is the top half of an unglazed scarab with lines in the white composition marking the body and shaping the head. Half the threading hole remains.

[UC 1196]
Length 1·5 cm.

The central scarab is glazed bright green. The base is flat but uninscribed. The moulding and glazing is stylised and unusually poor.

[UC 1367]
Length 1·0 cm.

The smaller scarab bead on the right is glazed blue and has a roughly scratched six-point crossed design underneath.

Frog Seals (ii)

The four faience frog seals are remarkably finely made. See mould [UC 2125].

The seal on the left has a bright blue glaze and is modelled with meticulous detail. It shows tensely flexed legs and the back is striped by lines made in the glaze. The longitudinal hole emerges under its raised head. The animal is expertly wrought both artistically and anatomically. On the seal is the feather sign, *šwt*, Shu (?).

The frog second to the left is glazed dark blue with an unevenly incised six-pointed cross on the seal. Its frog-like pose, although similar, is less distinct than the frog on its left.

Second to the right, the frog seal is of a blue-grey glaze. It has stripes in the glaze down its back. Two protruding eyes appear to have been applied separately; they have a glass-like appearance of patchy bright green (decay?). On the seal is a *nefer* sign.

48(i). Purple glazed faience cylinder and flat seals in the shape of scarab beetles. (Tallest 2·5 cm.)

[UC 1177]
Length 1·0 cm.

[UC 23659]
Length 1·0 cm.

[UC 1176]
Length 1·0 cm. P. *T/A*, pl. XVII (329).

48(ii). Frog seals. (H. 1 cm.)

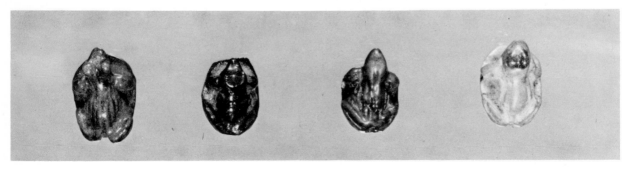

[UC 2127]
P. *T/A*, pl. XVII (328).

For comparison see . E. Riefstahl, A.E.G. and G., pl. 11, No. 25, Brooklyn Museum.

On the right, the particularly frog-like seal is glazed bright green with added brown eyes suffused with green below the brown suggesting glass and decay as in the example on the left. The threading hole emerges as on the others, under the head, but in this example the base is rounded in front making a platform under the hole which is between the flexed front legs. On the seal is the *šwt* feather, Shu (?).

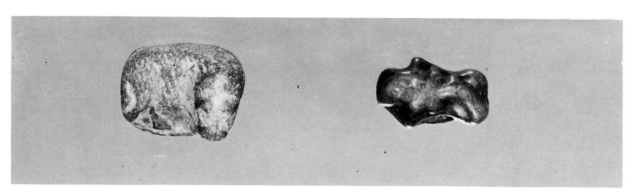

48(iii). Animal seals. (Longest 1·7 cm.)

[UC 1203]
Length 1·7 cm.

[UC 1828]
Length 1·5 cm.

Animal Seals (iii)

The recumbent bovine creature on the left has a chalk-like grey-mauve glaze covering it, possibly once purple. The seal is uninscribed.

On the right is a clumsily-shaped scorpion on a base, perhaps for the purpose of a seal design, but left uninscribed. The design is confused by the thick glaze and further blurred by the threading hole which is across the head.

FAIENCE TILES AND INLAYS

Lit. P. *T/A*, pp. 27/28, paras. 61/2. Comparisons: *City of Akhenaten*, Parts I, II and III (two volumes).

The thirty-eight examples in this plate of faience inlays, and tiles with inlaid designs, are from typical Amarna scenes. They cover a range of techniques sometimes all used in the same piece. Besides those fallen from walls, columns and probably lintels and door jambs, some of the heavier tiles may have been in floor scenes and some of the smaller ones in furniture.

Top Row

[UC 412]
Width 10·0 cm. Lit. J. Samson, *C/A III*, p. 228, pl. CVII (6).

On the heavy tile, top left, in which blue "water" lines and green lotus leaves are inlaid on a ground of white glaze, the edges of the lotus petals are incised, and their tips painted, brown. On the top right edge of the fragment part of a yellow inlay remains. The tile is heavy and a centimetre deep and suggests a floor tile. The back of it is unglazed.

[UC 542, 1279 and 1648]
Height 3·0 cm. to 3·5 cm. Depth 14·0 cm. to 15·0 cm. Lit. P. *T/A*, pl. XIX, 481–488. Comparison: Muller, A.K. K. & G., pl. 133.

On the three cornflowers in the top row centre the green calyxes and violet-blue petals are glazed front and back. The incised lines shaped on the calyx, and straight but fanning out for the petals, are only on the front. The right example is slightly convex and thicker than the other two. All appear to have been inlays.

[UC 1696]
Width 3·5 cm. Depth 1·0 cm. Unpublished.

The fragment of cornflower on the second right, with incised green calyx and incised blue striped petals, is a smudgily glazed inlay with a flat back. The front is convex as though to project from a wall.

The tile on the top right corner has green leaves, and possibly a fruit (persea?) on the left, inlaid into a bluish-white ground. The veins of the leaves and fruit are painted brown, and the yellow stems edged with brown paint. The right edge of the tile is finished and shaped for inlaying. The back is shaped but unglazed.

Second Row

The triangular yellow fragment second left of the second row is from a bright yellow tile with an unusually high glaze. Spiky leaves of raised green glaze are edged with brown paint; the shapes of the stem and branch are incised on one side and outlined in brown on the other. The back is unglazed.

Third left of the second row the fragment has a small half-green flower, the white half possibly left unglazed; it is on a bluish-white ground. Olive green leaves and the stem are outlined in brown. This fragile delicate tile has a white glazed, curved top. The back is unglazed with grit adhering, possibly from a sandstone background.

Centre of the second line is the top curve of a thin, shaped tile. The finished top edge continues along the inward curve on the right, down to the break. The papyrus heads bend elegantly with the shape of the tile. The white background is smudged with brown, possibly from the paint with which the stamens are shown; the green heads of the flowers are also painted on but the green stems are inlaid. The back is unglazed, with the finished edges bevelled.

[UC 413]
Width 6·7 cm. Depth 1·0 cm. Lit. *Cat. Ancient Egyptian Art, Burlington Fine Art Club*, p. 31 (2), pl. XL, London, 1922.

[UC 452]
Width 4·5 cm. Unpublished.

[UC 24288]
Height 3·6 cm. Width 2·8 cm. Unpublished.

[UC 437]
Height 4·0 cm. Unpublished. Translation by Professor Fairman.

VI. Fragments of faience tiles and inlays of fruit, flowers and from figures. Mosaic fragments in the bottom row. (Tallest H. 7 cm.).

The rounded bunch of grapes second from the right is one of many such clusters of grapes of varying sizes. They are mostly glazed blue, although there are green ones. Some are flat at the back for inlay; others have a hole pierced through the top for use as a hanging decoration. This example is rounded, with two halves joined, but like many others, the top half of the back is cut away, presumably to fit against another shape.

[UC 23260]
Length 3·0 cm. Lit. P. *T/A*, pl. XIX (441-48).

The thin fragment of bright blue glaze below the grapes is a piece of glazed decorated surface, or a tile. The incised pattern could be a flower or part of an Aten ray and hand. The back is unglazed.

The papyrus head, on the right of the second row, is an unusual inlay. The head of the flower is thickened and glazed at the top, to stand out from a surface. It fans out from the bottom, deepening from the middle to half a centimetre in depth at the top. Incised lines ridge the green glaze, following the shape from top to bottom, with brown dots painted at the top. The top edge is finely finished with a glossy red-brown glaze. The back is unglazed, except for an overlapping green rim, formed around the unbroken edges from the front green glaze. This colour is also smudged into the red-brown top.

The fragment of convex lotus below the papyrus is a raised flower of coarse glaze work. The leaves are glazed green; the petals of blue-white are tipped with dots of dark blue glaze. The back is glazed white, blue-green, and at the top a thick yellow layer. It would project if inlaid.

Third Row

The fragment of "daisy" tile, on the left of the second row, is one of many similar tiles found by Petrie from the walls of the "Coronation" Hall of the central palace. This fragment has the coarse, gritty, green glaze which is typical of them, with the unglazed recessed circles for the white daisy inlays, and the unglazed back. Between the inlays blue flowers with black edges are painted on the surface. In this fragment they have raised yellow glazed centres and brown painted stems. The top edge is finished for inlaying. A broken white daisy with yellow centre is laid into the left recess.

The two kneeling figures in the third row are bound foreigners. On the left is a blue glazed figure of a kneeling Asiatic (?) and on the right a red glazed figure of a kneeling Nubian. Possibly they are both inlays from furniture, as both figures are flat at the back which is glazed.

In the centre of the third row is part of a red glazed royal hand. This perfectly fashioned and highly glazed piece suggests a scene in which a royal figure is offering to the Aten or conferring honours on a courtier. The thumb and three fingers are raised in *bas-relief* against a ground of the red tile, which is as highly glazed as the fingers except for the spaces between them where the surface is matt. The nails are separately added in white glaze. On the thumb the nail is but a white strip. Behind the thumb the top surface of the tile is a centimetre thick and highly glazed. At the tip of the thumb the highly glazed edge turns down and continues obliquely to the break below it. The back of the tile is also glazed but with a less high finish and it is cross hatched presumably to increase the purchase on a wall; gritty sand adheres to it, perhaps from a sandstone wall.

Right of the central inlay are three red glazed hands. The two flat, smaller hands are probably inlays of Aten hands from the ends of inlaid rays. They are glazed on the flat back, and at the wrists for placing them beside the adjacent shape. The top hand with traces of white now between the fingers is deeper and more rounded. It is glazed overall and suggests the hand of a princess.

The two red glazed poppy petals for inlay on the right of the third row are both glazed at the back. They are decorated with different techniques.

The left one has the black tip painted on it and the white dots inlaid; the right has the part of a circle inlaid with white glaze.

Fourth Row

The triangular red tile, left of the fourth row, is a background inlay tile with a slightly raised green bud inlaid in the centre. It is one of those described by Petrie as making a garland of flowers and buds on a red ground. The base is broken; the back is glazed.

[UC 899]
Height 6·0 cm. P. *T/A*, p. 28, para. 61, pl. XIX (487).

The fragment of lotus inlay tile, second left of the fourth row is, like the other tile, an example of a colourful lotus pattern on a red ground. In this the inlaid green leaves of the flower surround the diamond-shaped white petal which is tipped with purple-blue; the red background is left only in the one inverted triangle visible at the top edge. The back is unglazed.

[UC 1559]
Height 6·0 cm. Comparison with one from a house, *C/A II*, p. 21 (26/286), pl. XXX (3).

The small red triangular tile, third left, is another from a garland against a red ground. The green lotus bud tipped with yellow glaze at the base is inlaid in the centre of the triangle, and at the top of the bud blue glaze is inlaid in a line on the left. Where they occur there are usually two of these inlaid lines dividing the calyx, in recesses made by raised lines in the mould. The back is glazed.

[UC 1553]
Height 3·5 cm. P. *T/A*, pl. XIX (487).

The fragment of tile inlaid with blue flowers in the centre has a bluish-white ground. Both the blue flowers (cornflowers?) and the green stems are inlaid and empty shapes show where other inlays have been dislodged. The back is unglazed.

[UC 24289]
Width 3·5 cm. Unpublished.

On the lotus tile, second right of the fourth row, the inlaid green glazed leaves are slightly raised. They spring from a yellow glazed base. The petals are part of the white ground, their shapes being incised. They are slightly "brushed" with blue around the edges, against a white ground. The edges of the tile are glazed. On the unglazed back are two small rectangular mortises and the remains of a third for inlaying and fitting this tile into a scene.

[UC 908]
Height 7·0 cm. Muller, *A.K.K. & G.* pl. 125 c.

Right of the row is the edge of a tile on which the base is painted with dark brown to represent Nile mud (?). It has the trunk of a palm tree rising from it, painted red with brown painted spikes. Trace of brown painted leaves (?) show in the top right corner. The right edge of the tile is finished.

[UC 790]
Height 5·2 cm. Unpublished.

Bottom Row

Left of the bottom row are two "blue" crowns for inlays on the King's head, their size suggesting they come from a multi-coloured composite figure inlaid in furniture. They both have the shaped edge (at the bottom of the plate) for round the face, and the ridge across the crown. Both have incised circles and both are a pale lilac-blue glaze resembling the colour of two of Nefertiti's crowns in the Collection, one of which is an inlay. There are stone reliefs with spaces for the inlays of crowns, wigs, flowers and the sun's disk, and faience shapes for inlaying them in the Collection: but of any delicate inlaid furniture at Amarna only such fragmentary pieces as these remain, for which Tutankhamen's furniture offers a parallel.

[UC 1558, 1251]
Height 3·0 cm. and 1·0 cm. Comparisons: *C/A I*, p. 121, pl. XXXIV (1) and (2). Similar crown, *C/A II*, pl. XXVIII (6).

The red glazed inscription, bottom row, third left, is a thin fragment of surface from a dark red glazed tile. It is rough at the back. Part of the disk (?) is above the *'ankh*; a vertical column line is on the right, and two lines at right angles on the bottom left. The lower finished edge is part of a circle.

[UC 23690]
Height 3·0 cm. Unpublished.

Three fragments of red glaze in the centre of the bottom row are inlaid

[UC 683, 685 and 687]
Width 6·0 cm. to 2·6 cm. Unpublished. Comparison: Muller, *A.K.K. & G.* pl. 199a and 199b.

with uneven yellow rhomboids and solid blue diamond shapes. The top two fragments are glazed red on both sides. Both are glazed at the back, the longer one with red, the shorter one with white. They could be part of the head and body of a snake for inlaying in a scene. The head shape is 1·2 centimetres deep; the shorter piece is 0·7 centimetres deep. The larger piece below them is broken on all edges, and suggests part of a cushion or footstool in an inlaid scene resembling the background to the two princesses in the Ashmolean mural from their home. It is only glazed on the surface, the back being rough or broken red tile.

[UC 607]
Width 2·0 cm. Unpublished.

The fragment of coloured mosaic in the bottom row, second right, is inlaid with a dark blue triangular network, itself inlaid with white circles; the "ground" of the tile appears to be equally small red inlays. In the top left corner is part of a turquoise diamond-shaped inlay; on the top right corner is half a similar diamond-shaped cavity. The piece could be from a foreigner's robe, and heralds the later inlaid shapes of mediaeval mosaics.

[UC 1636, 1783 and 2139]
Width 3·5 cm. to 1·5 cm. P. *T/A*, pl. XVII (304, 307, 309).

The three animal "offerings" on the bottom right corner are of a bovine head, trussed animal body, and the leg and foot of an animal, all in blue glaze. They are presumably from an inlaid scene of Aten offerings. The features on the head are painted brown.

FRAGMENTS OF FAIENCE TILES FROM POOL SCENES

The fifteen pieces of inlay in this plate show a variety of the techniques used in faience tiles at Amarna. The methods include varying the thickness of the glaze in shaping the pattern, as in the smaller of the two fish tiles; the use of "colour perspective" on the duck; and by supplementing inlaid pattern with painted and incised surface decoration on most of the fragments.

The subjects are reminiscent of the painted pavements, with fish and flowers in the pools, and fowl in the surrounding papyrus and reed plants. The tiles of reeds on the lower right of the plate are angled and shaped, presumably to fit around a central theme and maintain a flowing design without carrying the inlaid pattern over onto the next tile.

Bottom Row

[UC 419A, 420, 421]
Width 4·5 cm. to 4·0 cm. Unpublished.

All three tiles of water pattern left of the bottom row have a different colour scheme. The left example has dark blue water signs inlaid on pale blue glaze. It has a straight finished edge on the left.

The middle fragment has darker blue water signs laid into a white ground with the central yellow lotus base inlaid. The right edge is finished.

On the right fragment the water signs are alternate dark and light blue inlays with a dark brown edge, Nile mud (?) on the left.

Fish Tiles

[UC 472]
From nose to break, length 6·7 cm. From the back fin, width 6·2 cm. Unpublished.

Of the two fish tiles above the bottom row, the larger is a centimetre thick. It is of an unusually fine and smooth stone-like texture, with a thin glaze; this covers it, but the back is matt. The tile is broken perpendicularly from behind the back fin, which is chipped. The two curved brown lines from the bottom edge, gills (?), are deeply incised in the glaze and surface painted. The loop at the break and the stroke to the top like the line around the top are surface painted in brown. The eye is ringed with brown surface paint; the socket is recessed and glazed dark blue, with a raised brown glazed dot for the pupil; the mouth is realistically shaped as just open, by deep incision in the glaze, unpainted.

The smaller fish is only half the depth of the larger. The especially vitreous quality of the glaze covering it and the varied methods used on this tile give the fish a realistically underwater appearance. The fins and scales are painted brown. The folds around the eye are painted brown but also shaped by raised rings of glaze giving an effect of flesh. The eye is both painted and shaped. It is ringed with brown surface paint; the yellow glazed eyeball is raised, and an incised line surrounds the brown pupil. The stippling under the eye is of brown painted dots. The mouth is indicated both by incision and painting. The piece is glazed top and bottom but not at the back. The break cuts the tile behind the underneath front fin. A side fin is realistically painted on.

[UC 476]
Length 5·0 cm. Width 4·0 cm.
Unpublished.
Comparison: Muller, *A.K.K. & G.,*
A, 122a, 122b.

VII. Coloured faience tiles, a duck, fish and reeds from pool scenes. (Tallest H. 7·9 cm.).

Second Row

On the head and body of the duck, second from the top on the left of the plate, the beak is broken, and only the front half of the bird remains. On it is an example of colour perspective by the use of warm and cool colours. The yellow wing is a slightly thicker glaze than the grey-blue breast feathers and is separated from them by an incised line, but the raised effect of the wing is largely from the use of the warm yellow over the cool blue. The body feathers are painted in brown and the eye is painted. The head feathers are also painted, but they are rippled, presumably by dragging the viscous glaze. A blue-white glaze covers the edges, but the back is thickened by a deposit, apparently from the background into which it was set.

Top Row

The edge of the fragment of tile on the top left is slightly curved. All the

[UC 509]
Height 4·3 cm. Width 4·3 cm.
Lit. *Cat. Ancient Egyptian Art, Burlington Fine Arts Club,* p. 31, pl. XL (g), London, 1922.

[UC 24287]
Width 3·7 cm. Unpublished.

[UC 483]
Width 3·5 cm. Unpublished.

[UCC 425]
Height 4·0 cm. Unpublished.

[UC 435]
Width 4·0 cm. Unpublished.

[UC 438A]
Width 3·2 cm. Unpublished.

[UC 445]
Width 2·5 cm. Unpublished.

[UC 424]
Height 5·0 cm. Lit. *Cat. Ancient Egyptian Art, Burlington Fine Arts Club,* pl. XL (h), London, 1922.

[UC 423]
Height 6·0 cm. Unpublished.

[UC 426]
Height 7·9 cm. Unpublished.

pattern, the green papyrus head reaching to the edge, its brown calyx, and the dots around the edge are painted on blue-white ground. The back is whitened and has a bevelled edge at the top for inlaying.

The fragment, second right of the top line, has a glazed slightly curved top edge. The green leaves are inlaid into the blue-white ground but the brown grass (?) between the leaves is painted on. The back is unglazed with a bevelled edge for in-fitting.

On the top right is a nearly square fragment of thick corner tile, with a finished top and right edge. The green leaves are inlaid and the brown decoration painted. The back is rough and unglazed, but the blue-white ground from the front partly covers the sides.

Second Row

The fragment of tile on the left of the second row is broken all round, but the base of the flower at the top and the hollow for another on the left show the techniques were varied. The green base of the flower and the red-brown calyx and the green stems are all inlaid. The brown outline of the stems is painted in grooves at the side of the inlaid green strip. The unexplained brown line left of the top flower is painted decoration, perhaps one of the rare examples of a misplaced stroke. The white ground is recessed where the flower is missing on the left. The back is thinly glazed with white.

The small fragment with stems on its right, the second row, is broken all round. It has two inlaid green stems outlined in brown. Between them another is outlined in brown without the inlaid green strip. On the left are two painted brown "spear" leaves. The background is a blue-white. The back is unglazed.

The small fragment of tile with leaves and flowers on the right has all edges broken except the top. The green leaves are inlaid but all the brown decoration surface painted. The top edge is bevelled for inlaying at the back, which has been glazed white.

Third Row

The two triangular pieces of reed tiles, in the third row, are an unusual shape. In the smaller, central, triangular fragment there is a finished edge on the left which is angled to the right, possibly to a point like the piece on its right. The green stems and flower heads are inlaid but the stamens painted on the surface. The back is glazed a blue-white.

The larger triangular tile on the right-hand side is clearly shaped for inlaying as a triangle. The back is unglazed, with one edge bevelled and one cut or moulded straight. The green flowers and stems are inlaid; the brown outlines are incised and painted and the stamens only surface painted. The ground is a greyish colour, possibly discoloured like the tile in the right corner. The back glaze is also a greyish white.

Bottom Row

The tile with a finished base-line in the bottom right corner has another finished edge turning up on the right, to the break. The back is unglazed. Both finished edges and the unglazed back have a grey gritty substance adhering. The background is an off-white, pearl-like glaze, perhaps from undue heat, as the back and broken right edge of the tile have been burnt. All the green stems are inlaid, but the red-brown basal sheath is painted on the surface.

NOTE ON AMARNA MOULDS

In Petrie's description of the thousands of red clay moulds he brought back from Amarna he writes that he rejected large quantities of the commonest, but amongst the hundreds in the Collection are many variations for the innumerable faience inlays and amulets. In some a part of the unglazed composition base remains; in others the colouring of the object made in them can still be seen. A number, especially where the design is small or the recess deep have a line across the edge of the clay to give more purchase when prising out the small "positive". In many the thumb and finger marks are left in the clay from its shaping when damp. Apart from the technical interest of how the intricate tiles and *minutiae* were made, there is information to be gained from the moulds which supplements that from the amulets; they also show the figures of the gods that were made for the populace alongside the Aten symbols. The small selection here shows some unexpected designs, and demonstrates, notably in the seals, contact with the Near East and the Aegean.

Where moulds are published by Petrie in *Tell el-Amarna* a reference is given; otherwise most are unpublished.

Plate VIII

Lit. P. *T/A*, pp. 25-30, pls. XIV to XX. Comparisons: *City of Akhenaten*, Vol. 1, p. 170, pl. XIII; Vol. II, pp. 114-117; pl. XLIX; Vol. III, p. 182, pl. C.

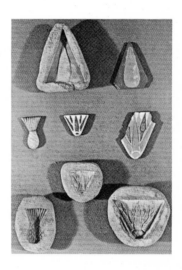

Facsimile of Colour Plate VIII. See p. 69.

Lit. P. *T/A*, p. 28, pl. XIX.

MOULDS WITH RELEVANT FAIENCE OBJECTS

The four moulds in this plate with relevant faience examples show various ways of making glazed tiles. At the top, the triangular mould has the shape of a lotus bud raised in the centre. This is for a tile similar to the one on its right, with the green bud set into the hollow made by the raised shape in the mould. The colour remains in many of the moulds where the red tiles were made as backgrounds for the coloured lotus garlands set into them. There are examples of the separate white petals and green faience lotus buds and leaves in the Collection, as well as moulds in which they were made.

The mould on the bottom left for an inlay of a cornflower has a faience example above it. Of the two lotus moulds, the bottom right is an example of a raised pattern, the other is recessed; above them are two inlaid lotus designs.

Red colouring remains in the triangular mould with a raised central bud on the top left of the plate. The red faience tile beside it has a green bud inlaid, in a hollow made by a similar mould. The green bud has two inlaid blue lines at the tip, making a point and suggesting the divisions in the calyx. The basal tip is painted yellow. The tile is glazed front and back.

The mould for a separate cornflower inlay, on the bottom left of the plate, could have made the faience example above it. The recess of the mould is 4·3 centimetres and it has the incisions for the usual shapes on the calyx and lines for the petals of the flower. The faience example is 4 centimetres long and shows the moulded markings on the green glazed calyx and violet petals.

The mould with a raised lotus design, bottom right of the plate, is for the typical lotus tile. The raised pattern has three outer leaves, at the centre and at each side; they run from the top to the raised elliptical base at the bottom.

[UC 1711, 1712]
Recess in mould, height 6·3 cm. Tile height 6·0 cm. Lit. P. *T/A*, pl. XIX (459). Comparison: Muller, *A.K.K. & G.*, Bud, pl. 133.

[UC 1647, 23637]
Lit. P. *T/A*, pl. XIX (481) (2). Comparison: Muller, *A.K.K. & G.*, pl. 133.

[UC 1710, 885]
Mould recess, height 4·8 cm. Faience
lotus, height 6·0 cm. Lit. P. *T/A*,
pl. XIX (458). Comparison: Muller,
A.K.K. & G., A, 125a, 125b, 126b.

[UC 1713]
Lotus recess, width 3·0 cm. Unpublished.

[UC 1715]
Width 3·3 cm. Lit. P. *T/A*, pl. XIX
(456).

The three petals each side of the central leaf are also raised.

In the faience example on its right, the three full length green outer leaves are inlaid in the hollows left by such a mould; one long diamond-shaped blue petal is inlaid each side of the central leaf, with a yellow diamond-shaped petal on each side of it. The ground is white. The yellow base is also inlaid in the hollow made by the mould

The centre mould with a recessed lotus design with three green leaves and a base has the usual number of three petals each side of the central leaf. The faience "positive" would have the lotus design raised from the background.

In the centre of the second row the small lotus-design spacer is a stylised example of three inlaid leaves, with one petal each side of the centre, and an inlaid base. All the inlays are purple in the white ground. At the back of the spacer there is a ridge across the top with five holes for the threads from a necklace, with another at the point of the spacer for them to be gathered through and presumably knotted.

MOULDS OF ROYAL AND RELIGIOUS SYMBOLS

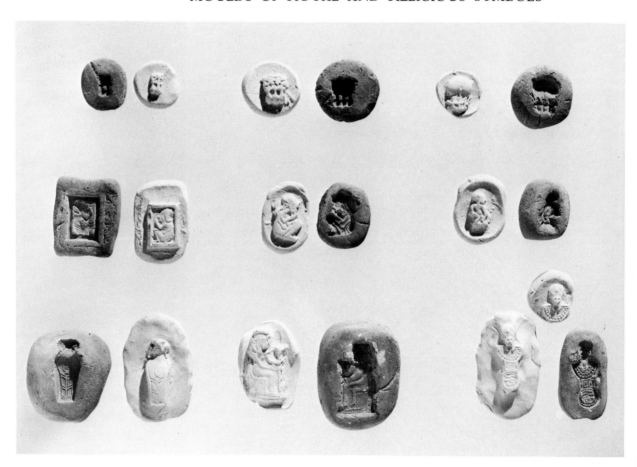

49. Red clay moulds for faience amulets of royal and religious symbols. (Tallest H. 4 cm.).

[UC 2021]
Height 1·0 cm. to 1·2 cm.

[UC 2028]
Height 1·5 cm. P. *T/A*, pl. XVII (251, 250 and 254).

The nine moulds in this plate are of amuletic symbols with royal or religious significance.

Top Row

Left of the top row, the design is of two *nfr* signs pendant from the *wḏ3t* eye. Beside it, in the centre, are three *nfr* signs from two eyes aligned as though in a face. Right of the top row, three *ankh* signs are pendant from the disk which has a raised uraeus in the centre.

94

Centre Row

The mould on the left and in the centre of the second row are both of a figure in the infantile position with knees drawn up and finger to mouth. The figure on the left, surrounded by a rectangle, faces right. It wears the *shendyt* kilt, and the side-lock of youth apparently over a shaven head. In the centre, facing left, is the small crouching figure of the King. He wears the blue crown with the uraeus in front and streamers behind, a necklace and the *shendyt* kilt. Hayes wrote of these designs possibly representing the King as "child of the Aten" and notes that in the Metropolitan Museum, the faience examples are only glazed blue. In this Collection, there is a red and blue faience figure in this pose. In the Ashmolean Museum, there is a similar small figure, glazed yellow.

Right of the second row is a naked, babyish figure facing right. It has a large head and bent legs.

Left of the third and bottom row is a cobra raised to strike. It is incised in detail. The body is moulded in depth and suggests it was for a faience cornice, perhaps on furniture, rather than to wear. The eyes and mouth are clearly modelled, and it has the V-shaped pattern on the body like the cloisons on bejewelled uraei. Above this pattern and below the head is a cartouche with the King's *pre-nomen Nfr-ḫprw-rꜥ w-n-rꜥ*. The amulet of this form to be worn is without the inscription.

Bottom Row

In the centre of the bottom row is an enthroned queenly figure facing left. She holds the papyrus sceptre before her and what is probably the *ꜥankh* in her right hand near her knee. A diadem surmounts the vulture head-dress, reminiscent of the God's Wife of Amen assumed by royal heiresses in the XVIIIth Dynasty and her left breast is bare over her sheath-like dress. Although without a surmounting head-dress, the figure also suggests a link with Hathor.

Right of the third row is the most precisely detailed of all the Amarna moulds. On the head of the cat goddess Bast, and between her upright ears, is the disk with uraeus in the centre. A lappet each side of her neck covers part of the deep, ornamental collar she wears; this forms the top of the *menat* symbol that is continued below it in the usual shape and highly decorated.

MOULDS FOR A CROWN, A SEAL AND FIGURES OF GODS

Top Row

On the top left corner is a mould for Nefertiti's crown. It has the straight front line to rise from the Queen's brow and the flap which lies over the cap-band in front of her ear. The surface is covered with blue circles with a dot in the centre as on the King's blue crown.

The same decoration is on two faience examples in the Collection, of the Queen's tall crown, both of which are glazed a bluish-grey. One has a flat back and straight sides, probably moulded for an inlay.

The other is slightly curved as though from a composite statuette.

[UC 2003]
Height 2·0 cm.

[UC 2004]
Height 2·0 cm. P. *T/A*, pl. XVII (271 and 272). W. C. Hayes, *Scepter of Egypt*, II, pp. 290, 291, N.Y., 1968.

[UC 2006]
Height 1·4 cm.
P. *T/A*, pl. XVII (275).

[UC 2177]
Height 2·5 cm. Depth 0·5 cm.
P. *T/A*, pl. XVII (319).

[UC 2016]
Height 3·0 cm. Width 1·5 cm.
Lit. P. *T/A*, pl. XVII (284).

[UC 24312]
Height 2·7 cm. Unpublished.

[UC 2050]
Height 1·2 cm. Width 1·4 cm.
P. *T/A*, pl. XVII (258).

[UC 24271]
Width 2·5 cm.

[UC 24270]
Diameter 4·0 cm.
Two glazed war crowns are on colour plate VI

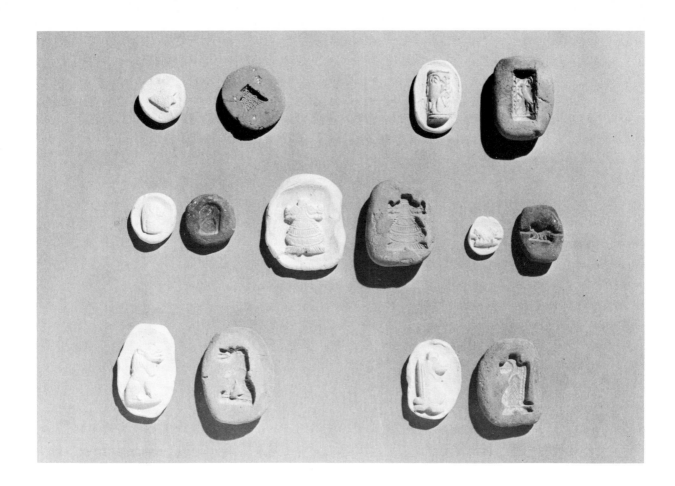

50. Moulds with the plasticine 'positives' of a crown, a cylinder seal and five gods. (Tallest H. 3 cm.).

[UC 2133]
Length 2·5 cm. Width 1·4 cm. P. *T/A*, pl. XVI (181). Comparison: *C/A III*, pl. LXXXIII (154)

[UC 2014]
Height 1·5 cm. Width 1·2 cm. P. *T/A*, pl. XVII (276).

[UC 24335]
Height 2·7 cm. Width 2·0 cm. P. *T/A*, pl. XVII (295).

Top right is a semi-circular mould for half a cylinder seal. The design is of an ibex (?) facing left; it stands on its hind legs with forelegs resting on the branches of a tree from which it seems about to nibble. The animal has strong curved horns, a large ear and a short, upturned, stumpy tail. It is clearly shown as male. The mould has a ridge top and bottom of the design, the latter forming the line on which the animal stands. The faience example, top left of plate 48, has a rounded rim each end, which would be made by this shape mould, and both are designs with foreign attributes.

Second Row

Left of the second row is the profile head and shoulder of a figure facing left. The eye and eyebrow, prominent nose and the mouth are clearly shown. The ear is large, and the long straight wig which falls front and back of the shoulder to the end of the design, is as though it were tucked behind it. Over the rounded shoulder, the rows of a large collar are incised; this is not shown in the drawing of an otherwise similar mould by Petrie. The mould has been blackened by smoke.

Centre of the second row is a two-sided creature with identical profile of head, body and foot facing each side. There is a fragmentary bright blue faience example in the Collection which fits into the double feet and lower part of the body, although the detailed design on the body is different. The head consists of a stylised long crocodile-like jaw with a circle and a central dot for the eye and nostril, joined by a line. Teeth are shaped in the open jaws. The body is covered by decoration between four upward curving lines which, with the shape of the body, widen as they descend. In the top and

96

bottom rows are circles with dots in the centre; the middle row has parallel upward stripes swinging outwards at the sides and these are echoed in the ribs of the large, flat, out-turned feet.

Right of the second row is a two-headed bovine animal or a presentation of two animals with heads in opposite directions. On the heads are horns and long ears and below the head two legs, presumably the front ones. Across edges of the mould is a horizontal line usually for prising out the faience shape, in this case possibly to preserve the heads of the very small design.

Bottom Row

Left of the bottom row is the mould of a seated animal facing left. It has long crocodile jaws, a prominent bulging eye high on its head, and a leonine mane behind big ears and over the front and back of the shoulders. A powerful rump is incised with lines suggesting fur or hair and the squatting pose with two forefeet in front is feline. There is a suggestion of Am-Mit in the expectantly open jaws of the creature and its compound characteristics.

Right of the bottom row, an animal facing left has the enlarged abdomen of Tauert, but the effect is less benign. The jaws are like a crocodile, and the shape with the projecting spine resembles hippopotamus goddesses with crocodile heads. A network of lines crosses the body and oblique stripes cross the perpendicular line down the projecting spine which ends in a tail above the back foot. Two flat feet are shown turning outward in a frontal view. A shape for the threading hole rises from the head.

[UC 2136]
Height 1·0 cm. Width 1·3 cm.
P. *T/A*, pl. XVII (306).

[UC 2159]
Height 3·0 cm. Width 1·8 cm.
P. *T/A*, pl. XVII (300).

[UC 2157]
Height 3·0 cm. Width 1·7 cm.
P. *T/A*, pl. XVII (296). Comparison: Budge, *From Fetish to God in Ancient Egypt*, p. 86, London, 1934.

Inscriptions

LIMESTONE SCARAB OF AMENOPHIS IV

This ceremonial scarab resembles in size and style those issued by Amenophis III to commemorate certain events, but in complete contrast, its content is religious. On it, Akhenaten as a young king faces right. He is seated on his right leg with his left knee raised and his arms uplifted to what were two large Aten cartouches, in the pose of the god Shu upholding the disk. The King wears a uraeus on his "bag" wig and under his right shoulder is part of

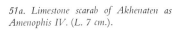

51a. Limestone scarab of Akhenaten as Amenophis IV. (L. 7 cm.).

98

the streamer from it. His necklace is a stylised semi-circle. The *shendyt* kilt is carved on the figure, below which is a large *nb* sign stretching nearly the width of the scarab. In front of him is a cartouche with his *pre-nomen*, and behind him his early throne name in another cartouche.

On the under surface, the left edge, part of the right edge and all the top of the scarab is chipped away. The damage is mostly to the surface stone, the top half taking most of the Aten names. Of the left Aten cartouche, only the bottom right corner remains with the reed and disk from the Aten name. At the base of the right cartouche the *3ḫt* is intact; level with this on the right are fragments of *nb pt*, at the end of a column of inscription.

The design is a striking parallel to that on the alabaster stela of the same scale in Berlin, where the Aten names are complete and in the early form. The significant difference is that, unlike the stela where the King is called Akhenaten, on the scarab his early name—*'Imn-ḥtp nṯr ḥk3 w3s*—Amenhotep, ruler of Thebes, is in the cartouche behind him. This has been rubbed to an ivory smooth concavity, presumably in an attempt to erase the association with Amen, as no damage has been done to his pre-nomen—*nfr-ḫprw-rˁ wˁ-n-rˁ*—in the cartouche in front of him. On the Berlin stela, Nefertiti's cartouche follows his name behind him where the scarab is broken away

[UC 2233]
Early Amarna period. Limestone. Length 7·0 cm. Width 5·0 cm. Lit. W. M. F. Petrie, *Scarabs and Cylinders with Names*, p. 27, pl. XXXVI (1), London, 1917. Comparison: *Catalogue Agyptisches Museum*, Berlin, p. 67, pl. 745, Inv. No. 2045.

51b. The head, back and legs of the scarab beetle on plate 51a. (L. 7 cm.).

but where there would have been room for it.

The carapace of the beetle is carved in detail; the eye is emphasised and the legs striated. A hole is bored longitudinally through it.

In 1917, Petrie included this scarab in his book *Scarabs and Cylinders*, but he gives no provenance for it. Presumably it was bought, but use of the King's early name suggests Thebes.

QUEEN TY'S SEAL

On the under surface of this limestone seal the central cartouche enclosing the royal name "Ty" is flanked on both sides with a spirited horse surmounted by a lizard—*ˁ3 sšmwt* (?). The carving is life-like and deep. The whole carved area is surrounded by an oval line. On the reverse the stone is roughly hewn into a raised spine which, although clumsy, would help to grasp the seal when

[UC 376]
Provenance: Amarna. Limestone. Length 16·5 cm. Width 6·5 cm. Depth 6·0 cm. J. Samson, *C/A III*; an impression on pl. CVIII.

52. *A seal for making a clay impression with Queen Toy's name in the centre and the signs for many horses either side. (L. 16·5 cm.).*

stamping the imprint. Since the inscription describes Queen Ty, as "rich in horses", this seal could belong to the time of her visit to Amarna in year 12 and have been used to seal the wet mud clamped on the bolts of her stables. The deep cutting leaves a bold impression of raised shapes in *bas-relief*, resembling those on the mud sealings of the outermost door of Tutankhamen's tomb.

A CARVING OF PART OF THE EARLY ATEN NAME

[UC 069]
Amarna. Chalky limestone. Height 8·0 cm. Width 6·0 cm. Unpublished.

The carving of "*Re-Harakhty lives*" from the name of the Aten used before year 9, is in shallow sunk relief (*en creux*) with ornate surface detail. In the groove made for the surrounding rope of the cartouche are faint traces of red from the thin rods of faience once inlaid. There are examples of such curved faience rods of varying widths in the collection.

The inscription *ʿnḫ Rʿ-Ḥr-3ḫty* is finely carved. The eye and beak of the falcon are incised in detail and the cap-like head feathers end at a line dividing the neck from the wing. The overlapping upper-wing feathers are followed by the straight ones at the end which overlap the long tail feathers. Those on the belly and thighs are finely chiselled. The disk worn by the falcon and those in the *3ḫt* signs have the uraeus raised in the centre front. The *ʿnḫ* hangs from the *3ḫt* signs, and one specifically carved stands in front of the bird. The surface of the chalky limestone has been worked to give a smooth flat facing.

100

53. A detailed carving of the falcon in part of the early form of the Aten name. (H. 8 cm.).

THE INTERMEDIATE FORM OF THE ATEN NAME

There are many examples of the conventional spelling of the early and late names of the Aten on inscriptions in the Collection. But there are also two examples of a transitional form in which the *Ḥr* is written phonetically. Professor Fairman pointed out the rarity of this, known only in its complete form on a mould for a faience cartouche in the Berlin Museum. The two examples in this Collection show for the first time that the second cartouche of this intermediate form is identical with that in the later form of the name.[1]

One example is in a double cartouche on the upper arm of a red quartzite figure in sunk relief. The forearm bends upwards from the elbow and is presumably a royal figure offering to or worshipping the Aten.

The spelling from right to left is:— *ꜥnḫ rꜥ Ḥr-ꜣḫty ḥꜥy m ꜣḫt m rn.f m itiꜣ m itn*.

The second example is from an alabaster stela near the "roll" at the top. The hieroglyphs are incised and filled with blue paste or "frit". There is one complete pair of Aten cartouches with the Aten names and the remains of two more cartouches on the broken left edge of the fragment.

The spelling in the complete cartouches is from left to right:— *ꜥnḫ rꜥ Ḥr-ꜣḫty ḥꜥy m ꜣḫt m rn.f m itiꜣ m itn*.

On the left of the fragment, the broken cartouches show the same full spelling of *Ḥr-ꜣḫty* but written from right to left. In the top cartouche the *ḫ* remains and *m ꜣḫt*. In the lower cartouche, the *ꜥnḫ rꜥ ꜣḫty* and the *ḥ* with part of the *r* and the *ḫ* below it.

Lit. [1] H. W. Fairman, *C/A III*, p. 183; J. Samson, *idem*, p. 231, pl. CVIII.

[UC 098]
Provenance: Amarna. Red quartzite. Height 6 cm.

[UC 351]
Provenance: Amarna. Alabaster. Height 6·5 cm.

54a. Two rare examples of the intermediate spelling of the Aten name. (H. 6·5 cm., 6 cm.).

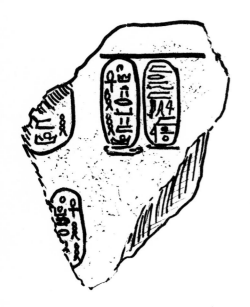

54b. Tracing of the intermediate form of
the Aten name as on plate 54a. (H. 6·5 cm.
and 6 cm.).

THE COREGENCY OF AKHENATEN AND SMENKHKARE

For the first time on plates 55A and 55B and 55C (Cairo), the eight significant pieces of a private stela recording evidence of the poorly documented
coregency between Akhenaten and Smenkhkare are published together. Of
the seven fragments found by Petrie, the four which make up the top right
corner with the double cartouches of the Kings on the obverse face, were not
joined when the stela was published previously.[1] The eighth piece, found in
1934, is from Cairo. It is the bottom, right corner and joins the border on the
obverse side. On the reverse is a portrait of the private owner of the stela.[2]

Carved on fine limestone, the stela is in the shape of a false door. On the
obverse, a small section of the torus roll and cavetto cornice remains above
the raised, right border. This is carved in sunk relief with lotuses arranged in
floral cones and offerings of fish. The carving is superior to that in the
recessed central area. In this, at the top right corner, are two pairs of cartouches placed as in a coregency.

The first pair contain the *nomen* and *pre-nomen* of Akhenaten: *Nfr-ḫprw Rᶜ
wᶜ-n-Rᶜ 3ḫ-n-'Itn* ("Beautiful are the forms of Re, the unique one of Re,
Akhenaten"). In the second pair are the names of Smenkhkare: *ᶜnḫ-ḫprw-Rᶜ
mry-wᶜ-n-Rᶜ* and *Nfr-nfrw-'Itn-mry-3ḫ-n-'Itn*, ("Living are the forms of Re,
beloved of the unique one of Re, beautiful are the beauties of the Aten,
beloved of Akhenaten"). In neither of the other two inscriptions recording
the names of the two kings in the coregency, does the actual name of Akhenaten appear. In the cartouches on Tutankhamen's box, the names are associated as *'Ankhkheprure* ᶜ *Mr(y/)) Neferkheprure* ᶜ("Living are the forms of Re,
beloved of (///) Beautiful are the forms of Re") and *Nfr-nfrw-ìtn mry wᶜ-n-R,*[3]

[UC 410]
Provenance: Amarna. Painted lime-
stone. Length of the right-hand border
in the Collection 25·0 cm. Full length
with the Cairo bottom corner 41·0 cm.
(Cairo, Vol. 14, JE 64959). Lit. [1]J.
Samson, *C/A III*, pp. 231-232, pl.
CVII (2 and 3), and pl. CVIII; [2] J. D. S.
Pendlebury, *idem*, p. 45 (34/42), pl.
LXXIII (8 and 9); H. W. Fairman,
idem, pp. 232-233. Comparisons:
[3]P. E. Newberry, *J.E.A. XIV*, p. 4/5;
[4]A. H. Gardiner, *idem*, p. 10; [5]N. de G.
Davies, *RTA, passim*.

103

*55a. Obverse of coregency stela of Akhen-
aten and Smenkhkare. (H. 25 cm.)*

*55c. Bottom right corner of the same stela
(Cairo). (H. 16 cm.)*

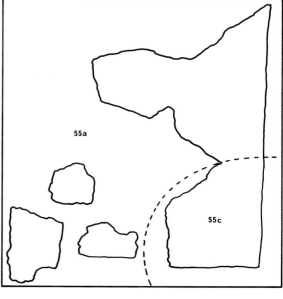

which corresponds to the association of the names on the graffito from the Theban tomb of Pere.[4]

Left of the cartouche with Akhenaten's *pre-nomen* are the faint remains of two larger cartouches with the inscription effaced (probably those of the Aten). Left of these, in the centre, is a poorly carved disk of the Aten with descending rays. It is flanked by the remains of the stereotyped inscription: on the right, facing right; two on the left, facing left.

Below this and the cartouches, the stone is missing but enough at the top of the scene remains to show the depth of the damage wrought. There are many scenes from Amarna where the King and Queen stand worshipping the Aten in the section of the picture which in this case has been destroyed.[5] In these, the cartouches that stand in the same relation to the scene as the names of the two Kings on this stela, belong to the King and the Queen, with the Aten. It might therefore be conjectured that, as in this case the cartouches of the King are beside those of his successor instead of by the Queen's name, the figure of the young King was also present below. The small fragment now found to fit between the cartouches of the two Kings and the Aten inscription shows that the cartouches, which were missing in the earlier publication of this stela, are almost twice the size of those of the King's cartouches and therefore almost certain to have been those of the Aten, and not of the Queen which, before the join was effected, it was thought could not be ruled out.

Three other relatable fragments in the Collection are shown on the left of plate 55a. On the obverse, the largest fragment is the lower left piece of the stela. In the corner made by the left border and the bottom edge is part of the recessed central area. In this, on a platform with two raised horizontal lines, is the right leg, and part of the left, of a figure facing right, and wearing a lightly incised robe or sash which flares out in a point behind the right leg. The small fragment on its right has a sandalled foot; this piece has a very broken surface. On the third fragment, above these, is part of a robe incised on the left of the abdomen of a figure also facing right. The navel is shown. Faint traces of red paint remain on the figure in all three fragments.

The bottom right-hand corner of the stela, now in Cairo, was found by Pendlebury in 1934 and later identified as part of this stela by Professor Fairman. On the obverse face of it, the right-hand border is continued, and part of the raised base. In the recessed area of this corner is the right edge of the platform with two raised horizontal lines as in the left corner of the stela shown on plate 55a. Standing on the right edge of this platform, carved in *bas-relief*, is a figure from the waist down. It faces left, there are sandals on the feet. At first sight it appears nude, but in front of it is a line on the stone which could be a beginning of the carving of a gown. The navel is shown; the hips and thighs are plump; the body bends forward from the hips as though offering to the Aten and the knees are slightly bent in this pose. In front of this figure is an unidentifiable shape which could be the leg of another figure, behind which a line is sketched which could also be the placing of the falling edge of a gown, and below this, by the ankle, is a short horizontal line that could be to mark the end of it or a sash.

On the reverse face of the top and left edge of the stela, formed by the four joined pieces, are the head and shoulders of a kneeling portrait of the

Plate 55c.

55b. Reverse of the top corner of plate 55a showing the owner of the stela.

owner, facing right. He is represented as a nobleman wearing the gold collar. The figure is carefully carved and some of the original coloured paint remains on the face and the wig which is bound by a fillet and crowned by a cone of unguent (?). His thin right arm, with two bracelets on the forearm, is lifted in acknowledgement; the hand is raised in front of his face (an incorrectly placed *left* hand) and his other hand is in front of it. The break in the stone is below the elbow and across the body under the shoulder.

Above the figure are traces of three vertical columns. The column on the left edge of the stela is so badly damaged that it is not possible to see if it had been finished or inscribed. The middle column reads: /// *Pr-n-p3-'Itn*, perhaps to be restored (*Pr-ḥʿy*)-*m-p3-'Itn*; and the inside column, of which only the lower part is preserved, finishes with *'ir ʿ*, perhaps for the title *'iry-ʿ3* "doorkeeper", although an unusual writing of it. On one of the three small fragments, the hieroglyphs for *pr-mrt-n* remain, with *t3 di'* (?) and *ʿ* (*ayin*) in the next column.

On the reverse of the Cairo piece, of the bottom left corner of the stela, is the lower part of the kneeling body of the owner. The pleats of his robe are shown passing diagonally behind his body, and around his hips is the pleated and fully flared kilt of the courtier. The chest and the body are finely carved but the foot on which the body rests is stylised. The toes rest on the top of the lower edge of the stela. In front of his knees are unexplained pleats hanging vertically.

106

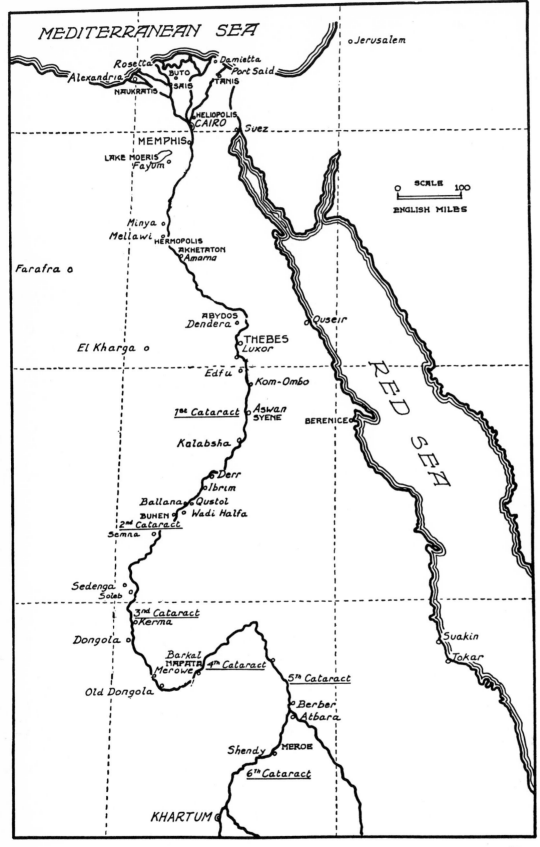

56. Map of Egypt.

The Nile Valley

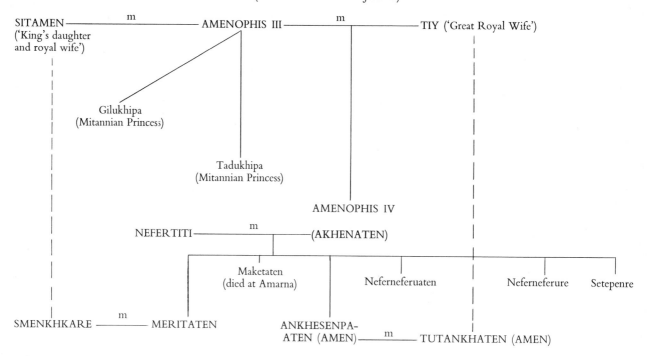

THE ROYAL FAMILY OF THE AMARNA PERIOD
(The dotted lines are conjectural)

The parentage of Smenkhkare and Tutankhamen is not known.

57. Chart of the Amarna royal family.

A brief note of Egyptian Dynasties and Rulers from 3100 to 30 B.C.

EARLY DYNASTIC PERIOD—First and Second Dynasties, *c.* 3100–2686 B.C.

OLD KINGDOM—The Pyramid Builders—Third to Sixth Dynasties, *c.* 2686–2181 B.C.

FIRST INTERMEDIATE PERIOD—Seventh to Tenth Dynasties, *c.* 2181–2040 B.C.

MIDDLE KINGDOM—Eleventh and Twelth Dynasties, *c.* 2040–1786 B.C.

SECOND INTERMEDIATE PERIOD—Thirteenth to Seventeenth Dynasties, *c.* 1786–1567 B.C. (The Hyksos Kings—*c.* 1674–1567 B.C.).

NEW KINGDOM—The Age of Empire, Amarna and the Ramesside Period—Eighteenth to Twentieth Dynasties, *c.* 1567–1085 B.C. (Eighteenth Dynasty, 1567–1320 B.C.).

LATE DYNASTIC PERIOD—Kings from Tanis, Bubastis and Napata, *c.* 1085–663 B.C.

SAITE PERIOD—Twenty Sixth Dynasty, 663–525 B.C.

PERSIAN KINGS—Twenty-Seventh Dynasty, 525–404 B.C. Twenty-Eighth to Thirtieth Dynasties, 404–343 B.C.

PERSIAN KINGS, 343–332 B.C.

MACEDONIAN KINGS, 332–311 B.C. (Alexander The Great, 332–323 B.C.).

THE PTOLEMIES, 311–30 B.C. (Cleopatra, 51–30 B.C.).